Birthday Cakes

Birthday Cakes

RECIPES *and* MEMORIES *from* CELEBRATED BAKERS

by Kathryn Kleinman

text by Carolyn Miller

CHRONICLE BOOKS
SAN FRANCISCO

Photographs by Kathryn Kleinman
unless otherwise stated.
Text by Carolyn Miller.
Cake styling by Stephanie Greenleigh.
Design by Michael Mabry.

Manufactured in China

Distributed in Canada by
Raincoast Books
9050 Shaughnessy Street
Vancouver, BC V6P 6E5

10 9 8 7 6 5 4 3 2

Chronicle Books LLC
85 Second Street
San Francisco, California 94105

www.chroniclebooks.com

Library of Congress
Cataloging-in-Publication Data:
Kleinman, Kathryn.
Birthday cakes : recipes and
memories from celebrated bakers
/ by Kathryn Kleinman.— 1st ed.
p. cm.
ISBN 0-8118-4019-0 (hardcover)
1. Cake decorating.
2. Birthday cakes. I. Title.
TX771.2.K58 2004
641.8'653—dc21
2003011792

For Adrienne with love
       from Auntie Kath

Birthday Cakes and Memories

29 White Mountain Cake JAMES BEARD

31 Orange Chiffon Cake MAIDA HEATTER

34 Gingerbread Cake with Chocolate Icing LAURIE COLWIN

36 Aunt Frances's Ricotta Cheesecake DONATA MAGGIPINTO

39 Heavenly Angel Cake MARION CUNNINGHAM

40 Frying Pan Chocolate Cake GEORGEANNE BRENNAN

43 Carrot Cake MAIDA HEATTER

46 Jelly Roll ROBBIN GOURLEY

49 German Chocolate Cake JOHN MARTIN TAYLOR

50 1-2-3-4 Cake ALICE WATERS

54 Fastest Fudge Cake ALICE MEDRICH

56 Becky's Birthday Cake TASHA TUDOR

58 Paw Paw's Birthday Caramel Cake with Caramel Frosting JAMES VILLAS AND MARTHA PEARL VILLAS

60 Grandmothers' Chocolate Cake EMILY LUCHETTI

63 Benoît's Upside-Down Caramelized Apple Tart PATRICIA WELLS

66 Grandmother Whitehead's Famous Texas Fudge Cake MARY OLSEN KELLY

68 Princess Cake GAYLE ORTIZ

74 Old-Fashioned Banana Spice Cake BRADLEY OGDEN

76 Le Kilimanjaro—Glace au Chocolat, Pralinée JULIA CHILD

79 Meyer Lemon Pound Cake STEPHANIE GREENLEIGH

8 Preface

10 Introduction

12 Baking Birthday Cakes

20 Decorating Birthday Cakes

80   Gold Cake with Grandma's Fudge Frosting   JIM FOBEL

82   Comforts Coconut Cake
     with Cream Cheese and Coconut Frosting   GLENN MIWA

87   Lindsey's Chocolate Cake   LINDSEY SHERE

88   Pavlova   RICHARD SAX

90   Cream Puffs with Lemon Filling   KATHLEEN STEWART AND DAVID LEBOVITZ

95   The Elvis Cake   MARIA BRUSCINO SANCHEZ

96   Magic Spice Cake with Penuche Frosting   ELOISE KLEINMAN

98   True Sponge Cake   MARION CUNNINGHAM

101 Beth's Very Berry Shortcake   BETH SETRAKIAN

102 Pineapple Upside-Down Cake   CINDY PAWLCYN

105 Lincoln Log Cake   SHERRY FALKNER AND ELIZABETH FALKNER

108 Pink Elephant Cutout Cake   STEPHANIE GREENLEIGH AND KATHRYN KLEINMAN

110 Easiest Hot Fudge Pudding Cake   EDITORS OF COOK'S ILLUSTRATED

113 Baby Cakes   FLO BRAKER

117 Green Cake (Vert-vert)   CREATED FOR CLAUDE MONET

119 Bittersweet Chocolate Pinwheel Cake   CARRIE BROWN

122 Birthday Cupcakes   STEPHANIE GREENLEIGH

124 Buttermilk Poppy Seed Bundt Cake   CINDY PAWLCYN AND DOROTHY PAWLCYN

127 Resources

130 Source Notes

133 Bibliography

134 Acknowledgments

136 Notable Birthdays

138 Templates

140 Index

144 Table of Equivalents

My love of birthday cakes started at a very young age. I grew up in a large family, with three brothers and three sisters. In our family, it was a tradition for every child to sit in the high chair on his or her first birthday and be presented with the birthday cake, which was placed on the chair's tray. As the family watched, the birthday child would explore the cake, first with trepidation, touching the frosting gingerly, then tasting it, then attacking the cake with abandon. My mom would remove the cake and cut it as soon as my dad had photographed the child, liberally smeared with frosting. The cakes were usually simple in design, a white or angel food cake with fluffy white frosting, or whipped cream flavored with vanilla and cocoa powder. My favorite was a white layer cake covered with seven-minute frosting, with sliced bananas and more frosting between the layers. My mom is now in her seventies, and today she bakes her special cakes for her grandchildren. ♦ Now, years later, with children of my own, I feel the same warmth each time we celebrate a birthday in my family. I love the ritual of making the cake, presenting it with glowing candles, whispering the secret birthday wish, blowing out the candles, and sharing the cake. Sometimes the cake might be made from a mix, or ordered from a bakery and decorated in a special way, or it might be the simplest homemade cake just sprinkled with confectioners' sugar, but the smiling face in the light of the candles and the fleeting instant of feeling that all is well in the world make the moment memorable. ♦ This book is a gathering of birthday cake recipes and stories, each of them unique and personal. I hope that these cakes and memories of wishes made on lit candles will inspire you to gather your loved ones around you and continue your own birthday traditions or create some new ones. ♦ The one who bakes the cake and gives it with love is the one whose wish always comes true.

—KATHRYN KLEINMAN

All birthday cakes glow, not just with lighted candles but also with promise and celebration. They glow in our memories of childhood and birthdays past, and in the commemoration of our passage through life. Each of us has one special day that marks our entrance into this world, and birthday cakes—sweet, ornamented, bright—honor that day like nothing else.

This book celebrates birthday cakes and what they mean to us. It offers recipes from well-known chefs and home cooks, as well as cherished memories of birthday traditions and special cakes.

The cake has symbolized life ever since wild grains were first crushed, mixed with honey, and formed into a disk. The long evolution of that first cake began with the use of fire for cooking, and progressed through the development of agriculture to the use of refined flours, sweeteners, and leaveners from yeast to eggs to baking soda and baking powder. Along the way, cakes were formed into symbolic shapes and lighted with candles to mark religious ceremonies and annual celebrations. The round cake signified, then and now, continuity, wholeness, and the circle of the seasons.

Today, every birthday cake is symbolic of many things: the life passage, the uniqueness of each person, the love of family and friends, the honoring of the traditions that bind us together as people, and the hope for a good future. The gift of a birthday cake, especially one made by the giver, is one of the most loving acts anyone can perform. The planning and preparation of the cake in secrecy, the darkening of the room for the presentation of the lighted cake, the singing of the birthday song, the wish and the blowing out of the candles are all pieces of a ritual that has been handed down through the centuries, and each time it takes place is a new celebration of life and love. *Birthday Cakes* was written to help that ritual to continue.

The "Birthday Cakes and Memories" chapter features thirty-eight cake recipes, many with an accompanying story explaining the special meaning the cake has for the contributor. It includes both classic cakes—favorite American cakes commonly served for birthdays—and unconventional cakes, for those who prefer something a little different. Like sugar crystals and confetti, other special family birthday traditions and memories are sprinkled throughout the book.

The wide variety of recipes in *Birthday Cakes* makes this an essential cookbook for anyone who wants to know how to make birthdays special. They vary from the simple and easy to make, such as a quick fudge cake from Alice Medrich (page 54), to the elegant and elaborate, such as the green pistachio cake made and served at Giverny by Monet's cook, Marguerite (page 117); and from traditional ones like James Beard's favorite birthday cake covered with fluffy white frosting and coconut (page 29) to imaginative and inspired ones, such as Julia Child's Le Kilimanjaro, a flaming ice-cream-cake mountain (page 76). You will find a cake here for everyone you know, from a baby celebrating a first birthday to an adult marking an important decade, and from toddlers to teenagers to extended-family members and significant others.

Whether you choose to make a modest cake dusted with confectioners' sugar and topped with fresh flowers, or a fancy creation covered with swirls of buttercream and decorated with frosting swags and rosettes, this book will help you to create bright memories for yourself and those you love. The "Baking Birthday Cakes" chapter contains all the basic information you will need to know to make successful cakes, while "Decorating Birthday Cakes" contains decorating ideas, a list of helpful decorating tools, and a glossary of decorations.

Baking Birthday Cakes

MAKING A CAKE FROM SCRATCH IS ONLY SLIGHTLY MORE DIFFICULT THAN MAKING ONE FROM A MIX; A CAKE
MIX ALREADY HAS THE DRY INGREDIENTS MEASURED AND COMBINED, BUT YOU STILL HAVE TO
BEAT IN THE EGGS AND LIQUID. A HOMEMADE BIRTHDAY CAKE IS A GESTURE OF LOVE, AND WORTH THE BIT
OF EXTRA EFFORT IT REQUIRES. THIS CHAPTER CONTAINS BAKING TIPS, LISTS OF BASIC INGREDIENTS AND EQUIPMENT,
AND A DISCUSSION OF FUNDAMENTAL BAKING TECHNIQUES TO HELP MAKE YOUR CAKE A SUCCESS.

BAKING TIPS

• Read the recipe through before doing anything. Follow the method for making the cake exactly as specified.

• Measure all the ingredients ahead of time and place them on the counter in order of use.

• Every few months, check that your oven temperature is correct by using an oven thermometer; the level of heat makes a big difference in the success of cakes.

• Read up on basic cake-making techniques, such as measuring flour, beating eggs and butter together, beating eggs and sugar together, and beating and folding in egg whites. The fine points of these procedures will make a huge difference in your baking success (see pages 17–18).

• Make sure the butter, milk, cream, whole eggs, and any other chilled ingredients are at room temperature; remove them from the refrigerator about 1 hour before baking (in a pinch, warm them slightly; see Butter, page 14, and Separating Eggs, page 18).

• Once you begin the cake-making process, proceed from step to step without delays. The following tip will help you do this.

• Preheat the oven for at least 20 minutes before putting the cake in the oven. When using glass cake dishes or dark-surfaced baking pans, reduce the oven temperature by 25°F. When baking at altitudes above 3,500 feet, increase the oven temperature by 25°F.

• Most basic layer cakes can be baked in different sizes and shapes of pans than the one specified in the recipe. The batter for two 8- or 9-inch layers will fill two 8- or 9-inch square pans, a 9-by-13-inch pan, or 24 muffin/cupcake wells. You will need to cook the 9-by-13-inch cake about 10 minutes longer, and the cupcakes about 5 minutes less. If in doubt, simply measure the capacity of the two different pans by filling each with 8-ounce cupfuls of water and comparing the capacity.

The important things to remember are that the batter should be 1 inch deep at the minimum, and that the batter should never fill the pan more than two-thirds full (with the exception of tube pans).

• Put the cake pans into the oven immediately after the batter has been mixed and added, especially cake batter made with beaten eggs or baking soda or baking powder. Handle cakes leavened only with egg whites with special care: Don't open the oven until very near the time the recipe says they will be done, as cold air can make them collapse. Follow the cooling and unmolding instructions for all cakes carefully, to keep them from deflating or cracking.

• Cakes and cake layers can be cooled, wrapped tightly in plastic wrap, and left to sit at room temperature for 24 hours before they are filled and/or frosted. Most unfrosted cakes also freeze well; wrap them in plastic wrap or aluminum foil, then place in airtight heavy-duty freezer bags. Allow them to defrost at room temperature.

BASIC INGREDIENTS

Baking Soda and Baking Powder
Check the shelf date on your packages of baking soda and baking powder to make sure they're still potent. This is especially important with baking powder. It's a good idea to buy very small containers of baking powder to help ensure its freshness.

Butter
Use the best unsalted butter you can find, preferably a European-style butter with a high butterfat content. When the recipe calls for room-temperature butter, make sure to remove the butter from the refrigerator an hour or two before cooking, depending on the heat of the kitchen. If you've forgotten, cut the butter into pieces, place them in a bowl, and set in a warm place, such as in the sun or in another bowl of hot water, for about 15 minutes.

Confectioners' Sugar
Also called powdered sugar, this fine sugar has a small amount of cornstarch added to it to keep it from forming lumps. Even so, it should be sifted before most

uses: Pour it into a fine-mesh sieve and force it through the sieve onto a sheet of waxed paper with the back of a spoon (don't use your flour sifter, as it will leave a sweet residue in the sifter).

Eggs
Use fresh large eggs at room temperature. (For egg whites, see page 18.)

Flour
Most of the cakes in this book use all-purpose flour; sometimes unbleached flour is specified, depending on the source of the recipe. A few cakes use cake flour, which is a fine soft-wheat flour. Be sure to use cake flour when it is called for, especially with foam cakes like sponge cake and angel food, or the cake will not rise the way it should. Cake flour should always be sifted before measuring.

Granulated Sugar
Use granulated pure cane sugar. Some cooks swear by baker's sugar, which is an ultrafine sugar that blends beautifully. You can make superfine sugar to use like baker's sugar by blending regular granulated sugar in a blender, or look for baker's sugar in grocery stores.

BASIC EQUIPMENT

Below is a list of basic equipment you'll need to make most of the cakes in this book. For a list of decorating equipment, see "Decorating Birthday Cakes," beginning on page 20.

Bowls
You will need a graduated set of heavy ceramic mixing bowls for beating batters and combining other ingredients, as well as a graduated set of stainless-steel bowls. Use these for melting chocolate and beating eggs over barely simmering water; they are easier to use and more versatile than a double boiler.

Candy Thermometer
For making some boiled icings.

Electric Mixer
Though you don't absolutely need a heavy-duty, or stand, mixer, they are most convenient, especially for beating eggs and sugar. A hand mixer or whisk can also be used.

Flour Sifter
Choose a triple sifter, with three layers of mesh.

Measuring Cups and Spoons
You will need a set of stainless steel cups for measuring dry ingredients and 1- and 2-cup Pyrex pitchers for measuring liquid ingredients. You should also have a set of metal measuring spoons.

Pans
Here is a list of the pans you will need to make the cakes in this book:

- Two 6-inch round layer-cake pans
- Three 8-inch round layer-cake pans
- Three 9-inch round layer-cake pans
- A 10-inch tube pan
- A 9-inch tube pan
- An 8-inch square glass baking dish
- Two 9-by-13-inch pans
- A 9-by-12-inch jelly roll pan
- An 11-by-15-inch pan
- A 12-by-15-inch pan
- A 6-cup Bundt pan
- A 12-inch cast-iron skillet (for making Pineapple Upside-Down Cake, page 102, or making a cake on a stove or campfire, page 40)
- A 9-inch tarte Tatin pan or cast-iron skillet
- Two baking sheets, preferably insulated or very heavy
- Muffin tins, for cupcakes

Look for heavy pans with straight sides for layer cakes; you can use springform pans, which are 2½ to 3 inches deep, rather than regular layer-cake pans, which are about 1½ inches deep. That way you can use one deep pan instead of two shallower ones, if you like, and split the cake horizontally, as this makes for a moister cake. Make sure the springform pans have a bottom that locks securely into place, unlike some false-bottom pans that can leak batter. See page 13 for how to vary pan sizes and shapes for a given recipe.

Parchment Paper and Waxed Paper
Use parchment paper or waxed paper to line the bottom of cake pans, and parchment paper for lining baking sheets. Use waxed paper for sifting dry ingredients onto.

Pastry Brushes
You will need two: one for butter and oil, and one for milk and other nonfatty liquids.

Plastic Dough Scraper
These flexible, curved plastic tools are not essential, but they are much more efficient than a rubber spatula for getting the last drop of batter out of a bowl.

Rubber Spatulas
Choose a wide one and a narrow one, at the minimum, and look for those with silicone blades, which are heat resistant.

Sieves
You will need a small fine-mesh sieve for dusting confectioners' sugar and cocoa, and larger sieves for sifting confectioners' sugar, for straining some mixtures, and for draining solid ingredients.

Oven Thermometer
Check your oven temperature every few months with a good oven thermometer, and adjust your baking time if necessary.

Timer
Look for a digital timer that has a magnetized clip on the back.

Whisks
You should have a tiny whisk about 1 inch wide for beating ingredients in small bowls, as for egg washes; and a sturdy, fairly stiff medium whisk, about 2 inches wide, for combining relatively heavy ingredients. To beat whipped cream and egg whites by hand, choose medium and large balloon whisks.

Wire Racks
Ideally, you should have at least four heavy wire cake racks for cooling cakes, either round or square.

Wooden Spoons
You will need at least two wooden spoons, one large and one medium in size.

Wooden Toothpicks/Skewers/Cake Tester
Any of these can be used to test a cake for doneness, though you might prefer a thin cake tester for delicate cakes like angel food, as it will leave a smaller hole.

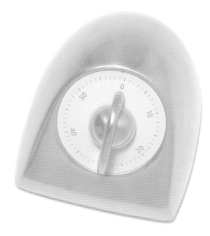

Basic Techniques

Preparing Pans

Follow the recipe instructions for preparing the pan(s). To cut paper rounds for the bottoms of pans, place the pan bottom on a sheet of parchment paper or waxed paper, draw around it using a pencil, and cut out the round with scissors. When making dense cakes that might stick to the pan, the pan is usually buttered, lined with a paper round, then buttered again (the first buttering keeps the paper round in place). Some instructions call for the buttered pan to be dusted with flour; to do this, sprinkle a couple of tablespoons of flour into the pan, turn it all around to coat the bottom and sides evenly, then invert the pan and tap the edge of it on the edge of the sink to knock out the excess flour. (See page 44 for a note on using bread crumbs in place of flour.)

Note: Most bakers prefer softened butter for greasing pans, but others swear by shortening (use nonhydrogenated shortening) or vegetable-oil cooking spray, so choose whichever one you prefer.

Arranging Oven Racks

Unless otherwise specified in the recipe, bake all cakes (and other baked goods) on the middle rack of the oven.

Staggering Pans

If you are baking two layer-cake pans at once, stagger the pans on the rack, then switch places halfway through baking and turn the cakes back to front as well, so they will bake evenly. Try to leave at least 2 inches between each pan, as well as 2 inches between the pans and the sides of the oven. When cooking three layer-cake pans at once, arrange two oven racks as close to the center of the oven as possible and place the third pan on the second rack so that it is not directly below either of the other pans. Switch the third pan to the back of the top rack halfway through, turning it back to front;

place the pan that was in the back on the top rack on the bottom rack, and turn it and the remaining pan back to front.

Melting Chocolate

Chop the chocolate into chunks roughly ½ inch in size and melt it in a double boiler over, but not touching, barely simmering water. You can also use a stainless-steel bowl set over a saucepan.

Measuring and Sifting Flour

If a recipe specifies sifted flour, it means you must sift the flour before measuring (the "presifted" label on the sack of flour doesn't count, because flour packs and settles as it sits). If a recipe doesn't specify sifted flour, measure the flour this way: Stir the flour in the container, using a spoon, to aerate it. Place your measuring cup on a square of waxed paper and spoon the aerated flour into it until it mounds and spills over. Level the top of the flour using a dinner knife. Use the same method to measure already-sifted flour, except of course you don't have to stir it.

Sifting Dry Ingredients Together

Sift dry ingredients together, in a triple-mesh sifter, onto a square of waxed paper. (The waxed paper allows you to transfer the dry ingredients and saves washing another bowl.) If there are leftover lumps in the top of the sifter, mash them through the top mesh with the back of a teaspoon, then sift them all the way through.

Separating Eggs

Eggs separate best when they are cold, but beaten whites mound higher when at room temperature, so remove them from the refrigerator 1 hour before using. You can also warm egg whites by setting the bowl in a larger bowl of hot water for a few minutes.

Beating Egg Whites

Make sure that the whites are at room temperature and free of any bits of yolk, and that the bowl and utensils are free of grease. If in doubt, wipe them with a paper towel dampened with vinegar. Choose a large, wide bowl to incorporate as much air into the whites as possible.

There are three stages of beating whites: (1) The egg whites form a light foam; (2) the whites form soft peaks that curve over on themselves; (3) the whites form stiff, glossy peaks that stand up well and curve just at the tips. Don't beat beyond this stage, or they will lose their shiny appearance and become dry and grainy looking.

Beating Sugar and Butter Until Fluffy

This step aerates the sugar and butter and makes it easier for the batter to rise. Beat sugar with softened butter for several minutes until the mixture is pale in color and light and fluffy in texture.

"Making the Ribbon"

Egg yolks and sugar need to be beaten for several minutes until they are pale in color and have thickened enough to "make the ribbon": When a beater or whisk is lifted, some of the mixture will fall off the utensil and form a slowly dissolving ribbon on the surface of the mixture in the bowl.

Stirring

Many recipes call for ingredients to be stirred just until blended; overstirring can affect the success of the cake. You will need to scrape the sides and bottom of the bowl and the wooden spoon 2 or 3 times during the stirring process to blend the mixture thoroughly.

Folding

To fold light and heavy mixtures together, cut down into the center of the mixture with the blade of a large rubber spatula held vertically, then scrape it along the bottom and side of the bowl. Turn the bowl a quarter turn and repeat just until the ingredients are blended.

Testing for Doneness

Follow the recipe instructions for doneness. Most cakes (but not all) are done when they just begin to pull away from the sides of the pan, a toothpick or cake tester inserted in the center comes out clean, and the top springs back when very lightly pressed with a fingertip. Use a timer and check for doneness at the earliest time the recipe indicates.

Cooling

Follow the recipe instructions. Most cakes need to sit in their pan on a wire rack for 5 minutes before they are unmolded; rich, dense cakes should sit for 10 minutes, while foam cakes like angel food should stay in their pan until completely cooled.

Unmolding

Run a small sharp knife around the edges of the pan. Place a wire cake rack on top of the cake and invert it; the cake should fall out. Tap the bottom of the pan a few times if it is reluctant. If you have used a paper round, the cake should not stick. (If unmolding a delicate cake, like a sponge cake, that will not be frosted, first place a dish towel over the wire rack so that it won't make indentations in the cake.) Invert the cake again, using a wire rack, so that it is right side up. If you have used a springform pan, remove the sides and then the bottom of the pan.

FIRST BIRTHDAY

IMAGINE THE MOMENT WHEN THE SENSATION OF HONEY OR
SUGAR ON THE TONGUE WAS AN ASTONISHMENT. . . .
I'M THINKING OF MY SON'S FIRST EXPERIENCE OF SUGAR: THE
ICING ON THE CAKE AT HIS FIRST BIRTHDAY. I HAVE
ONLY THE TESTIMONY OF ISAAC'S FACE TO GO BY (THAT, AND HIS
FIERCENESS TO REPEAT THE EXPERIENCE), BUT IT WAS
PLAIN THAT HIS FIRST ENCOUNTER WITH SUGAR HAD INTOXICATED
HIM—WAS IN FACT AN ECSTASY, IN THE LITERAL SENSE
OF THAT WORD. THAT IS, HE WAS BESIDE HIMSELF WITH THE
PLEASURE OF IT, NO LONGER HERE WITH ME IN SPACE
AND TIME IN QUITE THE SAME WAY HE HAD BEEN JUST A MOMENT
BEFORE. BETWEEN BITES ISAAC GAZED UP AT ME IN
AMAZEMENT (HE WAS ON MY LAP, AND I WAS DELIVERING THE
AMBROSIAL FORKFULS TO HIS GAPING MOUTH)
AS IF TO EXCLAIM, "YOUR WORLD CONTAINS *THIS*? FROM THIS
DAY FORWARD I SHALL DEDICATE MY LIFE TO IT."

—MICHAEL POLLAN,
FROM *THE BOTANY OF DESIRE*

Decorating Birthday Cakes

THE DECORATIONS FOR A BIRTHDAY CAKE CAN RANGE FROM A SIMPLE DUSTING OF
CONFECTIONERS' SUGAR AND SOME CANDLES TO A COATING OF MARZIPAN, FONDANT, OR MULTICOLORED FROSTING,
COMPLETE WITH SUGAR DÉCORS AND FRESH OR GLAZED FLOWERS. WHETHER YOU PREFER THE HOMEY
ELEGANCE OF A SIMPLE DOLLOP OF WHIPPED CREAM OR LAVISHLY PIPED FROSTING, THIS CHAPTER WILL HELP YOU TO
MAKE CELEBRATORY CAKES THAT LOOK AS GOOD AS THEY TASTE.

Decorating and Serving Tips

• When decorating a cake with confectioners' sugar or a glaze, or frosting a single-layer cake, place the cake on the cake plate right side up. When frosting more than one cake layer, place the bottom layer(s) on the cake plate upside down and the top layer right side up. If the layers are domed, cut off the domes with a long, thin serrated knife so the layers will stack evenly.

• To cut a cake layer in half, use a long, thin serrated knife. Make a shallow cut all around the perimeter of the cake. Cut through to the center, keeping the knife horizontal the entire time, then continue to cut while turning the cake. Make a small cut in the side of the stacked layers so that the cuts can be lined up and the layers will match after they are filled. Slide a cut cake layer onto a cardboard round, a pizza pan, or the bottom of a springform pan for transferring it to be stacked.

• If you want to decorate the cake directly on the plate rather than using a cardboard round (see page 22), use this method to keep the cake plate clean while the cake is being frosted: Cut four 3-inch-wide strips of waxed paper and place them on the edges of the plate at the 12, 3, 6, and 9 o'clock positions so that they overlap, and so that when the cake is placed on top of them, none of the plate is exposed. After the cake is frosted, pull each strip of paper out from under it.

• To keep cake crumbs from mixing with the frosting and spoiling its look, brush the cake lightly with a dry pastry brush to remove the crumbs. You can also make a crumb coat, or skim coat: First spread a very thin coating of frosting over the cake and let it set. Then spread with the remaining frosting, starting with the top of the cake. When using butter icings, dip the knife in hot water and dry it periodically to make a smooth finish.

• To lend stability to whipped cream used as frosting, baking expert Marion Cunningham recommends adding 2 tablespoons of nonfat dry milk per 1 cup of heavy cream prior to whipping.

• To use a pastry bag, fit it with the tip (and the coupler, if there is one), then place it, tip end down, in a drinking glass with the ends of the bag folded over the sides of the glass. Fill the bottom of the bag with frosting, using a spoon. Twist the end of the bag together to force the frosting into the bottom and out the tip, making the patterns you want. Simple patterns are fluted circles or circles of connected dots around the top and bottom edges of the cake, and rosettes on the top and/or the sides. To make a "drum" pattern, decorate the sides with tall X's using a small plain (writing) tip, then place rosettes of frosting inside each triangle.

• To light candles, use a long-handled match or, even better, one of the gas-fed lighters available in hardware stores and drugstores. Always start with the candles in the center of the cake. If using the long thin French candles, you can splay them out like a fountain for effect; this also makes them easier to light.

• Some heavy or sticky cakes need to be cut with a knife dipped in hot water for each cut, then wiped off. Angel food cakes should be cut with a serrated knife, preferably one with very fine serrations.

DECORATING TOOLS

Cake Turntable
This device makes it easier to frost a cake; a lazy Susan is just as good.

Cardboard Rounds
Rounds of cardboard, cut the same size of the cake, are helpful in transferring a decorated cake to a serving plate if you prefer not to decorate the cake on the plate. You can buy these at kitchen supply stores, or make your own.

Cake Plate/Stand and Cake Server
A large cake plate or stand and a cake server are lovely accouterments for any birthday cake. The larger the cake plate, the more room you have to decorate the rim with flowers, fruits, and/or leaves, if you like.

Icing Spatula
An icing spatula, which is a narrow, flexible metal spatula, works much better than a dinner knife for adding, spreading, and manipulating frosting. The palette knives found in art stores are perfect substitutes.

Pastry Bags
Pastry bags are indispensable for piping on frosting. You can fashion impromptu ones from parchment paper or typing paper, or even from plastic bags with one corner cut off, to do narrow plain piping, or you can use

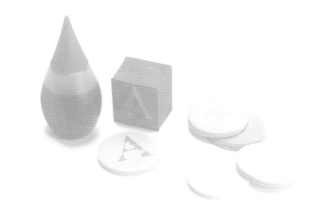

plastic-lined canvas bags that are fitted by dropping the tip inside the bag. But the most convenient pastry bags are plastic ones with plastic couplers that fit over the outside of the bag and screw on to hold the tip firm and keep frosting from escaping through the seam. These bags also allow you to use different tips on the same pastry bag, if you want to make different effects with the same color of icing. Look for Ateco cake-decorating kits in kitchenware stores or online (see Resources), and supplement them with extra pastry bags, couplers, and tips, which are also sold separately. You should have at least three bags and an assortment of tips (see below) for when you want to decorate with several colors and patterns of frosting.

Pastry Tips
The basic pastry tips are the writing tip, used for writing and narrow lines; the star tip, used for rosettes, and the scroll tip, useful for fluted borders and swags. You can use the star pastry tip to make icing rosettes on top of the cake, then insert a candle into each rosette. A ½-inch-wide plain tip and a bismarck tip are used to fill the cream puffs in Kathleen Stewart's and David Lebovitz's Cream Puffs with Lemon Filling (page 90).

DECORATING GLOSSARY

Candied Flowers

Candied violets and rose petals, available in kitchenware stores and specialty-food stores, are elegant cake decorations. Mix them with fresh violets and rose petals, or with tiny silver dragées for a lovely effect.

Candies and Cookies

Whether homemade or purchased, candies and cookies are easy ways to decorate a cake. Use macaroons, sugar cookies cut out in a variety of shapes, gingersnaps, ladyfingers, or any other cookie you like, pressing them into the icing on the sides of the cake. You can decorate a child's name or a "Happy Birthday" greeting on Necco wafers by using food coloring and a clean rubber stamp set to make the letters (see page 3). Seasonal candies are fun for birthdays near major holidays: Decorate a cake with Valentine candies for a February birthday, or use Christmas, Easter, or Halloween candies for celebrations on or near those times of year. And of course, candies like jelly beans, gumdrops, peppermints, and red hots can be used at any time. Crushed peppermints are a classic topping for a chocolate cake decorated with pink icing for a sweet-sixteen birthday.

Candles

Use the short birthday candles available in supermarkets, all in one color or in mixed colors for a child's cake or a festive adult one. For an elegant look, search out French birthday candles in kitchenware stores; these are usually about 8 inches long and very thin; they also come in a variety of colors.

The original candle tradition for children's birthday cakes was one for each year plus an extra one for good luck, though today most children want the exact number of candles for their age. Now that birthday cakes are traditional for adults as well, it's not always practical to have as many candles as the years being celebrated (and it's hard to blow out an entire forest of candles), so you may want to use one candle per decade, or just a token display of candles. At night, dim the lights before bringing the lighted cake into the room.

Chocolate Curls

Chocolate curls are good decorations for cake tops as well as for the rims of cake plates. To make them, run a vegetable peeler (preferably a Swiss peeler, which has a horizontal rather than a vertical blade) under hot water for a few moments, then dry it well. Scrape it over the top of a square of chocolate in a long stroke to create a thin curl.

Citrus Zest

Freshly shredded citrus zest makes a pretty garnish for cakes and/or the rims of cake plates. A zester, available in many supermarkets and kitchenware stores, has a rounded end with small holes for shredding the thin colored outer layer of citrus peels. Shredded zest will wilt and turn brown if made too far ahead, so add it just before serving.

Coconut

Shredded sweetened coconut, whether plain, toasted, or tinted, is a delectable decoration.

To toast coconut: Use either of the two methods for toasting nuts (see page 25). Watch the coconut carefully and stir it frequently to keep it from burning.

To tint coconut: Put the coconut in an airtight container with a lid or a heavy self-sealing plastic bag. Add a tiny drop of food coloring, close the container or bag, and shake to distribute the color.

Confectioners' Sugar and Cocoa

A light dusting of confectioners' sugar is all some cakes need, particularly rich ones like pound cakes. To dust, put a spoonful of confectioners' sugar in a small fine-mesh sieve and press it through with the back of a spoon while moving the sieve over the cake to dust it evenly. A dusting of cocoa, made using the same technique, is a nice addition to a pale icing, especially when the cake underneath is chocolate.

You may also want to dust the rim of a cake plate or individual dessert plates with either confectioners' sugar or cocoa, as a final embellishment.

For a patterned topping of confectioners' sugar on a dark cake such as gingerbread or chocolate, lay a paper doily on top of the cake and dust it evenly with confectioners' sugar, then remove the doily. The ambitious can

make stencils from stiff paper, such as kraft paper, for any number of patterns, including personalized ones. A quick and easy stencil is the first initial of the birthday girl or boy: Draw the initial, fairly large, on the stencil paper, then cut it out using an X-acto blade on a cutting mat. See also the stenciled crown on page 138.

Dragées, Colored Sugars, and Sprinkles

Supermarkets and kitchenware stores have a variety of edible cake décors to mix and use with abandon or to single out for special effect. Use large dragées (silver-colored balls) to spell out the birthday celebrant's name on the top of the cake (use tweezers to place them), or look for tiny dragées to sprinkle onto the tops and sides of cakes.

Food Coloring

The most common food coloring is the kind that comes in tiny glass or plastic bottles. Keep a selection in the four basic colors—blue, green, red, and yellow—so you can mix them as you like to make other colors. Take care to add food coloring to frosting in very small amounts. You can always add more to get the depth of color you want. When adding coloring to small bowls of frosting to use as piped decoration, dip a wooden toothpick in the coloring and then insert the toothpick in the frosting; mix and repeat until the color is as you wish.

Dedicated cake bakers prefer paste coloring, which comes in a wider range of colors. These are available from some kitchenware shops, or by mail order from confectionery companies (see Resources).

Natural food coloring can be made from vegetables, like the spinach coloring used to make the frosting for Monet's Green Cake (page 117). The liquid from cooking sliced peeled beets can be used to make red food coloring. Buttercream made with egg yolks will yield a pale yellow frosting, which will turn a pale peach color when a little red food coloring is added, and a very pale green when blue coloring is added. Experiment to make your own natural colorings; just be sure the coloring you choose doesn't add an odd flavor to the frosting.

Fresh Flowers, Leaves, and Fruits

Nothing is simpler or more beautiful than decorating a cake with fresh flowers, leaves, and/or fruits. Look around your garden or nearby fields for flowers in season, making sure that they have not been treated with pesticides and that they are edible (though your guests may not necessarily eat them). Make a nosegay of flowers to cluster on top of the cake in the center, sprinkle whole flowers or petals over the cake, and/or cluster blossoms and leaves on the rim of the cake plate.

Some of the best choices of flowers are roses and rose petals, violets and violas, calendula blossoms and petals, lemon and orange blossoms, mock orange blossoms, nasturtiums, and borage blossoms, which are bright blue and faintly cucumber flavored. Individual herb flowers, such as thyme and lavender, are good to

sprinkle over a cake, or use the whole blossom spikes to decorate the rim of the cake plate. Use the leaves of the above flowers to garnish the rim as well, especially violet leaves and small nasturtium leaves. Fruits that can be used include candied fruits, such as kumquats and cherries, or fresh fruits such as cherries, raspberries, and strawberries.

Rinse all flowers, leaves, and fruits briefly in cold water, shake them dry, and let them dry further on paper towels. Keep flower stems immersed in cold water until just before cutting off the stems and placing the flowers on the cake and/or plate.

Glazed Flowers, Leaves, and Fruits
A frosty glaze makes fresh flowers, leaves, and fruits even lovelier for decorating cakes and cake plates. To glaze, simply beat an egg white until it is frothy, then dip the cleaned item in the egg white, or brush the egg white on with a pastry brush. Lightly dredge in superfine sugar, then sprinkle more sugar over to cover any missed places. Let dry on a wire rack. Use the same day.

Marzipan
This thick, flavorful paste of ground almonds and sugar can be used to cover cakes, like Gayle Ortiz's Princess Cake (page 68), but it may also be used to make animals, fruits, and vegetables for cake decorations, such as the little carrots for Maida Heatter's Carrot Cake (page 43). Your imagination is the only limitation.

Nuts
Use whole blanched almonds or walnut or pecan halves to decorate cakes, placing them in a pattern. Or sprinkle slivered or sliced almonds, chopped pecans or walnuts, or whole or chopped pistachios over the top of a cake. To decorate just the sides of a cake with chopped nuts, frost the cake, then hold it up over a plate of chopped nuts with one hand; cup the chopped nuts in the other hand and coat the sides of the cake with them, rotating the cake to coat it evenly. Use nuts just as they come from the bin or package, or toast them lightly to add flavor and color.

To toast nuts: There are two methods of toasting nuts. The simplest is to toast them in a dry skillet, but you must watch them very carefully and stir them frequently, as they will go from toasted to burned very quickly. Toast them over medium heat just until the faintest bit of color begins to show; this will be accompanied by the fragrance of toasting nuts. Immediately empty them into a bowl to stop the cooking. Delicate nuts such as pine nuts and slivered almonds will toast much more quickly than harder ones like unblanched almonds. The second method is to spread the nuts in a jelly roll pan and toast them in a preheated 350°F oven, stirring them once or twice, for 5 to 8 minutes, depending on the nut. This takes a little longer, but the nuts are less likely to burn.

Whipped Cream
To make whipped cream, be sure the cream is cold before beating. Heavy cream will double in volume when whipped.

Birthday Cakes and Memories

This collection of cake recipes ranges from the beloved and familiar to the surprising and fanciful. It was gathered from professional chefs and master bakers, as well as some dedicated home cooks who love to make birthday cakes. This chapter includes most every kind of cake, from white, yellow, and chocolate (in many variations) to nut, carrot, and angel food, and ranges from traditional frosted cakes and fanciful creations to birthday fruit tarts, cream puffs, and ice cream cakes for nonconformists. All of the cakes are accompanied with recipes for frostings and decorating ideas, but many of them also lend themselves to variation and can be filled and topped with frostings from other recipes and decorated according to your own whims and desires.

White Mountain Cake

❀

IN *JAMES BEARD'S AMERICAN COOKERY*, THE LATE JAMES BEARD, KNOWN AS
THE FATHER OF AMERICAN COOKING, REMEMBERS HIS CHILDHOOD BIRTHDAY CAKES AND
HIS VERY PARTICULAR IDEAS ABOUT HOW THEY SHOULD BE FROSTED AND DECORATED.

*I have never forgotten my early birthday cakes. Blessed with an insatiable taste for coconut,
I always wanted a cake piled high with it. And since my birthday came in May, there were usually hawthorn blossoms
available to decorate the plate. I felt that candles ruined the beauty of the cake and was firm
about dispensing with the blowing out of candles ritual. These cakes, under their white icing and coconut, were
usually a sunshine or moonshine cake or a white mountain cake.*

—JAMES BEARD

MAKES ONE
10-INCH
TUBE CAKE;
SERVES 8 TO 10

½ cup (1 stick) unsalted butter at room
    temperature
1½ cups sugar
2½ cups sifted cake flour
3 teaspoons baking powder
¼ teaspoon salt
1 cup milk
1 teaspoon vanilla extract
4 egg whites

SEVEN-MINUTE FROSTING
3 large egg whites
¾ cup sugar
⅛ teaspoon salt
⅓ cup light corn syrup
1 teaspoon vanilla extract

MAKES ABOUT
5 CUPS,
ENOUGH TO
FROST ONE
10-INCH TUBE
CAKE

2 cups sweetened shredded coconut
Hawthorn or other blossoms for deco-
    ration (optional), see page 24

Preheat the oven to 350°F. Butter and flour a 10-inch tube pan; knock out the excess flour. In a large bowl, cream the butter and sugar together until light and fluffy. Sift the flour, baking powder, and salt together onto a sheet of waxed paper; repeat 2 times to incorporate as much air into the mixture as possible. Alternately fold the dry ingredients into the batter with the milk, beginning and ending with the dry ingredients. Stir in the vanilla to blend.

In another large bowl, beat the egg whites until stiff, glossy peaks form. Gently fold the egg whites into the batter.

Turn the mixture into the prepared pan and smooth the top to level the batter. Bake for 45 to 60 minutes, or until the cake pulls away from the sides of the pan and the top springs back when lightly touched. Let cool in the pan on a rack for 15 to 20 minutes before loosening from the sides and around the tube of the pan. Invert onto the rack, remove the pan, and let the cake cool completely.

To make the frosting: In the top of a double boiler, combine the egg whites, sugar, salt, and corn syrup. Set over simmering water and beat the mixture with a hand mixer for about 7 minutes, or until soft peaks form. Remove the pan from the water and stir in the vanilla. Continue beating until the frosting is stiff enough to spread.

Place the cake on a serving plate and frost by heaping spoonfuls of the frosting on the top and spreading it over the top and down the sides, making swirls and peaks. Sprinkle the coconut over the top and sides. Decorate the edges of the plate with blossoms and place a spray of flowers in the hollow of the cake, if you like.

Orange Chiffon Cake

福

MAIDA HEATTER, THE "QUEEN OF BAKERS," OFFERS THIS CLASSIC RECIPE
IN HER COOKBOOK, *MAIDA HEATTER'S CAKES*. A GOOD CHOICE FOR BIRTHDAYS, IT IS EASY
TO MAKE AND KEEPS WELL.

AMY TAN, AUTHOR OF *THE JOY LUCK CLUB*, REMEMBERS HER CHINESE FAMILY
CELEBRATING HER BIRTHDAY WITH A CHIFFON CAKE,
A VERY AMERICAN CONFECTION INVENTED IN CALIFORNIA IN 1927.

*In 1956, my parents had recently met another Chinese couple with two daughters, Sandy and Daphne,
and that family would later join with mine to create the real Joy Luck Club.
But in that year, for my and Daphne's fourth birthday and Sandy's second, we joined together for a party.
My brother, Peter, wearing his Davy Crockett outfit, exchanged his coonskin cap for a
birthday hat. Two neighborhood children were invited. My mother had made us a beautiful cake,
orange chiffon with confetti sprinkles and colorful sugary dots on top of a
whipped cream frosting. The cake looked absolutely American, round and with four birthday candles.
But the flavors and textures, chiffon and whipped cream, appealed to a Chinese palate
that prefers fresh fruit, sponge cake, and nothing too sweet or buttery.*

*In this picture, the table is set, the hats are on, and I am the grinning child who has been looking straight
at my father the entire time as he counted off, "One, two, three, say cheese…"*

—AMY TAN

**MAKES ONE
10-INCH
TUBE CAKE;
SERVES 16
OR MORE**

2 cups sifted all-purpose flour
1½ cups granulated sugar
3 teaspoons baking powder
1 teaspoon salt
½ cup tasteless vegetable oil, such as
safflower
7 large eggs, separated

Finely grated zest of 2 lemons
Finely grated zest of 3 deep-colored
oranges
¾ cup fresh orange juice
½ teaspoon cream of tartar
Confectioners' sugar for dusting or
Orange Buttercream Frosting (recipe
follows)

Place an oven rack in the bottom third of the oven. Preheat the oven to 325°F. Choose a 10-inch tube pan; it must not be nonstick, and it must be in two pieces: the bottom and tube in one piece and the sides in another. Do not butter the pan.

Sift the flour, sugar, baking powder, and salt together into a large bowl. Make a wide well in the center of the dry ingredients. Add, in the following order and without mixing, the oil, egg yolks, lemon and orange zests, and orange juice. Using a sturdy medium or large wire whisk, beat until smooth. Set aside.

In a large bowl using an electric mixer, beat the egg whites with the cream of tartar until they hold a stiff peak when the beater is raised. For this recipe, they must be stiffer than usual; when they hold a stiff peak, beat for 1 minute more. They should not be beaten until dry.

In 3 additions, fold about three-fourths of the yolk mixture into the whites. Then fold the whites into the remaining yolk mixture. Do not handle any more than necessary. (The yolk mixture is heavier; it will sink in the whites. To incorporate the two mixtures without additional folding, it may be necessary to gently pour the mixture from one bowl to another once or twice.)

CONTINUED

Gently pour the batter into the cake pan and bake for 55 minutes. Increase the oven temperature to 350°F and bake 10 to 15 minutes longer, or until the top springs back when it is lightly pressed with a fingertip. Immediately hang the pan upside down over the point of a funnel or the neck of a narrow bottle. Let the cake hang in the pan until completely cool.

To remove the cake from the pan, you must use a sharp knife with a firm blade about 6 inches long. Insert the blade at one side of the pan between the cake and the pan, inserting it all the way down to the bottom of the pan and pressing it firmly against the side of the pan in order not to cut into the cake. With short up-and-down motions, saw all around the cake, continuing to press the blade against the pan. Then, using a knife with a very narrow blade, cut around the tube.

Remove the sides of the pan. Then carefully, again pressing the blade against the pan, cut the bottom of the cake away from the pan. Cover the cake with a flat cake plate and turn the cake and the plate over. Remove the bottom of the pan and leave the cake upside down.

Dust generously with confectioners' sugar or frost with orange icing (as shown on page 30).

ORANGE BUTTERCREAM FROSTING (from Carolyn Miller): Prepare Buttercream Frosting (page 98), but in place of the vanilla, use 2 tablespoons thawed frozen orange juice concentrate and the grated zest of 1 orange. Makes about 2 cups, enough to frost 1 cake.

OUR VARIATION: To re-create Amy's cake, as shown on page 30, frost with Whipped Cream Frosting (page 95) and decorate with candy confetti and multicolored sprinkles.

Big Blue Roses

For birthdays, I was probably like most kids of my generation. We had large sheet cakes from the local bakery, spread with layers of lily-white frosting that probably didn't have a speck of butter in it. (It wasn't about flavor; it was about volume and the ability to stand up to any weather, and be presentable.)

Usually there was a spray of big blue roses made of icing in the corner of the cake. When the cake was sliced, we all wanted the flowers. I can still feel the way those sugar crystals crunched between my teeth and the rich, rich frosting left a layer of dubious fat in my mouth. Of course, I loved it all. But the bakery frosting was the best part. Even now, when I make classic buttercream for a cake, I am reminded of that bakery birthday cake frosting.

—David Lebovitz

Gingerbread Cake with Chocolate Icing

IN *HOME COOKING: A WRITER IN THE KITCHEN*, NOVELIST AND
SHORT-STORY WRITER THE LATE LAURIE COLWIN GIVES HER RECIPE FOR HER FAVORITE
BIRTHDAY CAKE, ALONG WITH AN ACCOUNT OF ONE OF HER BIRTHDAY PARTIES.

My birthday is a sort of makeshift affair. My favorite cake is gingerbread with chocolate icing, and I make the cake the night before. Sometimes I make two layers, and sometimes I split one. When the cake is cool, I spread the middle with a very, very thick layer of raspberry jam and stick the layers together. The top is spread with a thin layer of jam and the cake is left to stand, uniced, overnight. The next morning, I make a plain butter, sugar and chocolate icing . . . on which, at my daughter's insistence, sprinkles of various kinds—chocolate and multicolored—are festooned.

This year to go with the cake I made a plate of cheese buns—white bread dough rolled thin, stuffed with Gruyère, chopped scallions, black pepper and a little olive oil, scattered with chopped rosemary and baked in the oven.

The guests included two girls, seven and eight, a nine-year-old boy, two three-year-old girls (one mine, one my oldest friend's) and two baby boys, aged seven months and ten months, plus various parents.

"Don't give the baby any birthday cake," said the mother of the ten-month-old baby. "It's too spicy. It will make him cry."

"It's my birthday," I said. "Can't he have a taste?"

"Just icing," said his mother.

The icing was a huge success.

"Oh, give him a little cake," said his father.

"No!" said his mother. "It will make him scream."

I gave the baby a little piece of icing with cake attached. He began to laugh and pound his fist, which means "More!"

The babies all ate ginger cake. The three-year-olds ate cake and then attempted to pick off all the icing. The older children ate cake and cheese buns and then everyone helped clean up. By the time the last dish had been put in the dishwasher, the three-year-olds had been fed their suppers and given their baths. One was asleep in her bed and the other was in a taxi on her way to her bed. Every crumb had been eaten, the table had been wiped. The toys had been put away and there was a relative degree of order in the house. It was seven thirty, with plenty of time to finish the paper, read a book and send out for Chinese food.

Now, that's what I call a good party.

—LAURIE COLWIN

MAKES ONE
9-INCH CAKE;
SERVES 6

½ cup (1 stick) unsalted butter at room
    temperature
½ cup packed light or dark brown
    sugar
½ cup molasses
2 eggs
1½ cups all-purpose flour
½ teaspoon baking soda
1 heaping tablespoon ground ginger
    (for a very gingery cake; use less if
    you prefer)
1 teaspoon ground cinnamon
¼ teaspoon ground cloves
¼ teaspoon ground allspice
2 teaspoons lemon brandy or vanilla
    extract
½ cup buttermilk or milk with a little
    yogurt beaten in
Raspberry jam for filling and topping

MAKES ¾ CUPS,
ENOUGH TO
FROST 1 CAKE

CHOCOLATE ICING:
4 tablespoons unsalted butter at room
    temperature
¼ cup unsweetened cocoa powder
1 teaspoon vanilla brandy, vanilla
    extract, or brandy
1 cup sifted confectioners' sugar

Chocolate and/or multicolored sprin-
    kles for decoration (optional)

Preheat the oven to 350°F. Butter and lightly flour a 9-inch cake pan; knock out the excess flour.

In a large bowl, cream the butter and brown sugar together until fluffy. Stir in the molasses. Beat in the eggs, one at a time. In a medium bowl, combine all the dry ingredients and stir to blend. Stir the dry ingredients into the butter mixture. Stir in the brandy or vanilla and the buttermilk or milk mixture until well blended.

Pour the batter into the prepared pan. Smooth the top and bake in the center of the oven for 20 to 30 minutes (check after 20 minutes have passed), or until a cake tester inserted in the center of the cake comes out clean. Let cool completely in the pan. Run a knife around the edges of the pan and unmold the cake onto a wire rack.

Using a long, thin knife, cut the cake in half horizontally through the center. Spread the top of the bottom half thickly with raspberry jam. Place the top half on top and spread it thinly with raspberry jam. Let the cake sit out overnight.

To make the icing: In a medium bowl, cream the butter until fluffy. Stir in the cocoa powder, then the brandy or vanilla. Gradually stir in the confectioners' sugar to make a spreadable icing.

Frost the cake with the chocolate icing and decorate with the sprinkles, if you like.

VARIATION: This cake is also delicious with lemon icing. In place of the cocoa, add the grated zest of 1 lemon, 1 teaspoon lemon extract, and 1 tablespoon fresh lemon juice.

Lemon icing, I have discovered, must stand around for a while in order to bloom. At first taste, it is impossibly sweet, but after an hour or so it mellows into something suave and buttery.

Aunt Frances's Ricotta Cheesecake

A FAMILY RECIPE FROM DONATA MAGGIPINTO, A FOOD AND ENTERTAINING EXPERT, THIS
LIGHT, NOT-TOO-SWEET ITALIAN CHEESECAKE IS A GOOD ALTERNATIVE
FOR PEOPLE WHO DON'T CARE FOR TRADITIONAL BIRTHDAY CAKES. *NOTE:* YOU WILL NEED
TO START THIS RECIPE ONE DAY AHEAD, AS THE RICOTTA SHOULD DRAIN OVERNIGHT.

*Growing up in an Italian household, I learned that as we navigate through life's happy victories and
more sober vicissitudes, food is the constant companion. My Aunt Frances (still cooking up a storm at ninety!) has
been my inspiration, along with her light but luscious ricotta cheesecake. This creamy cake, studded with
bittersweet chocolate and laced with cinnamon, was always on our table for holidays and birthdays. You'll be happy
when it's on your table, too. As my Aunt Frances says as she pinches our cheeks,* Mangia!

—DONATA MAGGIPINTO

MAKES ONE
9-INCH CAKE;
SERVES 12

1½ pounds whole-milk ricotta

CRUST:
2½ cups all-purpose flour
⅓ cup sugar
¼ teaspoon salt
½ teaspoon baking powder
½ cup (1 stick) plus 2 tablespoons cold
    unsalted butter, cut into small pieces
1 large egg, lightly beaten with ¼ cup
    milk

¾ cup sugar
4 large eggs
1 tablespoon vanilla extract
⅓ cup chopped bittersweet chocolate
1½ teaspoons ground cinnamon
1 large egg beaten with 1 tablespoon
    milk and a pinch of salt for brushing

Line a large sieve placed over a bowl with 2 layers of damp cheesecloth and empty the ricotta into it. Cover the ricotta with plastic wrap and place the sieve and bowl in the refrigerator to drain overnight.

To make the crust: In a food processor, combine the flour, sugar, salt, and baking powder. Pulse once or twice to combine. Add the butter and process until the mixture becomes powdery. With the machine running, add the egg mixture and process just until the dough holds together. Turn the dough out onto a floured board. Knead gently and briefly just until smooth. Pat the dough into a disk, place it in a self-sealing plastic bag, and refrigerate for at least 1 hour.

Preheat the oven to 350°F. Butter the bottom and sides of a 9-by-2-inch cake pan.

In a food processor, process the drained ricotta until smooth and creamy. Transfer to a medium bowl and stir in the sugar. Beat in the 4 eggs, one at a time. Stir in the vanilla, chocolate, and ½ teaspoon of the cinnamon.

Reserve half of the pastry. On a lightly floured board,

roll the remaining pastry out into a 14-inch round. Fit the pastry round into the prepared pan, gently pressing it to fit, and allowing the pastry to hang over the edge. Pour in the filling and sprinkle with the remaining 1 teaspoon cinnamon.

Roll the reserved pastry out to a ⅛-inch thickness. With a pastry cutter or knife, cut it into ten 9-by-¾-inch strips. Brush with the egg mixture.

Moisten the rim of the dough on the pan with the egg wash. Attach 5 pastry strips in each direction, pressing the edges of the strips onto the rim to form a lattice. Trim the pastry around the pan, then gently press it down and off the top rim so that it rests within the pan.

Bake the cheesecake until the filling is set (the cake will jiggle slightly when you tap the side of the pan, but it should not move like liquid) and the pastry is just golden, about 50 minutes. Transfer the pan to a wire rack and let the cake cool completely. Unmold it by inverting it onto a flat plate, then reinverting it onto a cake plate so that the lattice faces up.

Heavenly Angel Cake

◯

MARION CUNNINGHAM'S FAMOUS VERSION OF ANGEL FOOD CAKE IS THE RESULT OF MUCH
EXPERIMENTATION AND TESTING. IT IS LOFTY AND DELICATE, PARTLY DUE TO
HER METHODS OF NOT OVERBEATING THE EGG WHITES AND OF ADDING A SMALL AMOUNT OF
WATER TO THE BATTER. HERE IT IS DECORATED WITH A COCOA WHIPPED CREAM FROSTING.

*I looked forward to making my son's first birthday cake, rather than buying one from a bakery.
As an overwhelmed working mother, however, I decided to use an angel food cake mix. I carefully followed the
directions on the box and baked the cake as instructed. To my dismay and horror, the cake
was not high and tender, but about three inches tall, dense, and chewy. I rushed back to the market to buy a different
brand of cake mix and started again. This time it worked. My baby boy had his first cake,
with one little candle aglow on the top. He loved his first taste of cocoa-flavored whipped cream frosting.
And I have the memory forever in my heart.*

—KATHRYN KLEINMAN

MAKES ONE
10-INCH
TUBE CAKE;
SERVES 10 TO 12

1½ cups sugar
1 cup sifted cake flour
1½ cups unbeaten egg whites (about 12)
2 tablespoons cold water
1½ teaspoons cream of tartar
½ teaspoon salt

1½ teaspoons vanilla extract
½ teaspoon lemon extract (optional)
½ teaspoon finely grated lemon zest
   (optional)
Few drops almond extract (optional)

Preheat the oven to 325°F.

Add ½ cup of the sugar to the flour and sift them together 3 times (use 2 pieces of waxed paper to sift back and forth on).

Put the egg whites in a large bowl and add the water, cream of tartar, salt, and flavorings all at once. Beat until barely stiff enough to hold a peak when the beater is lifted. Don't beat until the egg white mixture is dry (this is most important, because if the whites are too stiff, the air will be knocked out of them by folding in the remaining dry ingredients). Gradually add the remaining 1 cup sugar 2 tablespoons at a time, beating gently after each of the first few additions, then fold in the remaining additions. Gently fold in the flour mixture 3 or 4 tablespoons at a time until blended.

Spoon the batter into an ungreased 10-inch tube pan. Tap the pan sharply on the table a couple of times to break up the large air bubbles. Bake for 50 to 60 minutes, or until a cake tester comes out clean when inserted in the center of the cake. Remove from the oven and invert the pan to cool the cake upside down (this is important, because the cake will collapse if left to cool right side up). Let cool completely, then unmold.

COCOA WHIPPED CREAM FROSTING
(from Eloise Kleinman):

2 cups heavy cream
½ cup unsweetened cocoa powder
1 cup sugar
1 teaspoon vanilla extract

Place all of the ingredients in a deep bowl and stir gently with a wire whisk just until combined. Cover the bowl and place in the refrigerator for 15 to 20 minutes to chill the cream and allow the flavors to blend. When ready to frost the cake, use clean, dry chilled beaters and beat the cream mixture until it forms hard peaks.

To frost: First frost the inside of the hole of the tube cake. Place a little round cutout of cardboard over the hole and frost the rest of the cake. Serve immediately. Makes about 4 cups, enough to frost 1 cake.

NOTE: The intensity and sweetness of this frosting may be adjusted by using less sugar or cocoa.

Georgeanne Brennan

Frying Pan Chocolate Cake

Not all birthday cakes have to be perfect, made-from-scratch masterpieces. Sometimes, necessity can make a celebration just that much more special, as in food writer and cookbook author Georgeanne Brennan's account of making a birthday cake without an oven. Remember this technique for your own wilderness or car-camping trips.

I hadn't intended to make my stepson Tom's birthday cake in a frying pan, but I had no choice. We had set out early in the morning to ski cross country with friends to a wilderness cabin that had been loaned to them for the weekend. None of us had been there before, but we had directions. After skiing about three-fourths of a mile from California's Tahoe-Donner ski area, we were to follow a trail that led through the forest, and stay on it until we reached the cabin, six miles away on the edge of a stream.

I had only been cross-country skiing twice before, and never with a fifteen-pound pack of food on my back. After the first uncontrollable descent down the incline at the beginning of the trail, which terminated with me upended like a turtle on its back, I took off my pack and divided its contents among the others. The box of devil's food cake mix and the can of fudge frosting I tucked surreptitiously into my husband's pack, along with a box of blue birthday candles and two cake pans.

After many mishaps and adventures, we arrived at the cabin just at dusk, three hours later than anticipated. The cabin was one large room outfitted with a wood-burning range, a table, chairs, bookcases, and pantry at one end, and a series of bunk beds at the other, with a half-loft overhead. Gas lanterns were hung from the beams. I don't know why it had never occurred to me that the cabin wouldn't have electricity and gas.

There was a note on the oven that read, "Doesn't Work." Of course, we were all cold, wet, and hungry. We built a fire in the stove, and another one outside. I felt

terrible that Tom was going to have his birthday with no cake. When my eye rested on a large, heavy cast-iron frying pan, vague memories stirred of my grandmother telling me about how a Dutch oven could be used to cook anything. Exploration among the pans unearthed a lid that fit the frying pan. Assembled together, they looked very similar to the Dutch oven I had inherited from her.

I greased the frying pan with some of the butter I had brought and mixed up my cake batter as directed on the package: Pour 1⅓ cups water and ½ cup vegetable oil into the cake mix, add 3 lightly beaten eggs, and mix well. I poured the batter into the pan, covered it with the lid, and set it over the largest burner on the stove. The fire was roaring, and I left the rings on, afraid that if I set the pan directly over the flames it would burn the bottom of my cake.

After about 40 minutes, the cake was done, or at least it looked like it by lantern light. The top was firm to the touch and sprang back when I gently pushed it. I decided, though, that I wouldn't try to get the cake out of the pan. I took it off the stove and let it cool before spreading it with the chocolate frosting, then I put the lid back on.

At the end of the meal—huge porterhouse steaks we had hauled in, red wine, salad, and bread—I gripped the handle of the pan and brought my masterpiece to the table, now fully decorated with burning candles, which Tom blew out in one breath. We devoured the cake, which was moist and chocolatey, saving one piece for the birthday boy to have the next day.

—Georgeanne Brennan

MAKES ONE
12-INCH CAKE;
SERVES 4 TO 8

Butter for greasing skillet
1 box devil's food cake mix
Water, vegetable oil, and eggs as called
    for in cake-mix recipe
1 can chocolate frosting

Butter a 12-inch cast-iron skillet. In a large bowl, combine the cake mix, water, oil, and eggs. Beat with a whisk until smooth.

Pour the batter into the skillet. Place the pan on a burner on top of a medium-hot wood stove or on a grate over a low campfire. Completely cover the pan with a lid or inverted pan and cook for about 30 minutes, or until the top of the cake is dry and springy when touched with a finger.

Let cool. Spread with the frosting and add candles. Cut into wedges and serve directly from the skillet.

Carrot Cake

EVERYONE LOVES CARROT CAKE, AND THIS ONE, FROM BAKING GURU MAIDA HEATTER'S
BOOK *MAIDA HEATTER'S CAKES*, IS A GOOD CHOICE FOR LARGE BIRTHDAY CELEBRATIONS,
AS IT SERVES UP TO 20 PEOPLE. IT'S A PERFECT BIRTHDAY CAKE FOR ALL THOSE PEOPLE
WHO WANT TO HAVE THEIR SWEET TREAT AND EAT THEIR VEGETABLES TOO. MAIDA POINTS
OUT THAT THE CAKE IS ALSO FOOLPROOF AND CAN BE MADE AHEAD OF TIME.

MAKES ONE
9-INCH 3-LAYER
CAKE; SERVES
12 TO 20

1 cup (5 ounces) dark raisins
1 pound carrots (to make 4 cups
 shredded, firmly packed)
2 cups minus 2 tablespoons sifted
 all-purpose flour
2 teaspoons baking powder
1 teaspoon baking soda
1 teaspoon salt
2 teaspoons ground cinnamon
1 tablespoon unsweetened cocoa powder
4 large eggs
2 teaspoons vanilla extract
1 cup granulated sugar
1 cup firmly packed dark brown sugar
1¼ cups corn oil
1½ cups (5½ ounces) walnuts, cut into
 medium-size pieces

CREAM CHEESE ICING:
16 ounces Philadelphia-brand cream
 cheese at room temperature
½ cup (1 stick) unsalted butter at room
 temperature
1 teaspoon vanilla extract
2 cups sifted confectioners' sugar

12 to 20 walnut halves or marzipan
 carrots (optional), page 44

MAKES 4 CUPS,
ENOUGH TO
FROST 1 CAKE

Adjust 2 racks to divide the oven into thirds. Preheat the
oven to 350°F. Butter three 9-inch round cake pans and
line the bottoms with rounds of parchment paper or
waxed paper. Butter the paper and dust the bottoms and
sides with fine dry bread crumbs (see note); tap out the
excess crumbs and set aside.

Steam the raisins: Put them in a vegetable steamer or a
metal strainer over shallow water in a saucepan. Cover the
pan, place on high heat, and let the water boil for about
10 minutes. Uncover and set aside.

It is not necessary to peel the carrots; just cut off the
ends, wash them well with a vegetable brush, and drain or
dry them. They may be grated on a standing metal grater
or in a food processor. They may be grated fine, medium,
or coarse; I have used all these methods and found very
little difference in the cakes—no one was better than the
others. Measure and set aside.

Sift the flour, baking powder, baking soda, salt, cinnamon, and cocoa together and set aside.

In the large bowl of an electric mixer (or in any other
large bowl, with an egg beater or a wire whisk), beat the
eggs until blended. Beat in the vanilla, both sugars, and
the oil. Then, on low speed, add the dry ingredients and
mix just until incorporated. Stir in the carrots, raisins,
and nuts.

Pour the batter into the prepared pans. The solid ingredients have a tendency to mound in the center of the pans;
use the back of a teaspoon to distribute them evenly. Place
2 pans on one rack and 1 pan in the center of the other
rack—no pan should be directly above another. Bake for
35 to 40 minutes, or until the tops just spring back when
gently pressed with a fingertip and the cakes begin to
come away from the sides of the pans. If the cakes are not
baking evenly, you may reverse the pans, front to back and
top to bottom, after about 20 minutes, but I don't find it
necessary with this recipe.

CONTINUED

Remove from the oven and let stand for 2 or 3 minutes. Cover a pan with a wire rack, turn the pan and rack over, and remove the pan (do not remove the paper linings—they keep the cake moist—but if they come off by themselves it is okay). Cover with another wire rack and turn over again, leaving the cake right side up to cool. Repeat with the remaining layers. When cool, brush loose crumbs off the sides of the cakes.

Before you fill and ice the layers, freeze them for at least 1 hour, or until they are firm enough to handle (or they might crack). I like to freeze them overnight or longer and ice them a day or two before serving. If freezing them for an extended time, wrap them after they become firm. (If the layers have been frozen for a long time, do not thaw them before icing.)

To make the icing: In a large bowl using an electric mixer, beat the cheese and butter until soft and smooth. On low speed, beat in the vanilla and sugar, then beat on high speed for a few minutes until smooth.

To ice the cake: Prepare a large flat cake plate by lining it with 4 strips of waxed paper (see page 21). If you have a cake-decorating turntable, place the cake plate on it. Remove the paper from the cake layers.

Place one cold and firm cake layer upside down on the plate, checking to be sure that the paper strips touch the cake all around. Spread a thin layer (⅔ cup) of the icing evenly over the cake. Repeat with a second cake layer, then top with the third layer, also upside down. Use as much of the icing as needed to cover the sides of the cake, and then the top. You can work over this icing again and again. If you are using a turntable, take your time, work carefully, and use a long, narrow metal spatula to smooth the icing. Without a turntable, you will probably be better off swirling the icing a bit, but it is a thin layer and cannot be swirled deeply. Remove the paper strips by slowly pulling each one out toward a narrow end.

The cake can be left plain, or it can be decorated with a circle of nut halves or marzipan carrots around the top rim. If you decorate the cake with the nuts or carrots, do it immediately, before the icing dries, pressing them lightly into the icing to keep them in place. If using the carrots, place them pointed end in, green end out.

Refrigerate the cake for at least a few hours or up to 2 days. Serve it very cold, right from the refrigerator. Cut small portions; it is rich.

OUR NOTE: Years ago, Maida found a recipe for a European cake in a little brochure. The recipe called for dusting the cake pan with fine dried bread crumbs, the unflavored kind that you can buy at your local market. Ever since, she has coated her cake pans with bread crumbs instead of flour. The results have always been perfect—better than flour. You can use this technique for all recipes that call for buttering and flouring cake pans.

MARZIPAN CARROTS: Use one-third of the recipe on page 70 to make twenty-four 1¾-inch carrots by tinting some of the marzipan orange for the carrots and some green for the stems. Make these before you make the cake; refrigerate in airtight container for up to 1 month.

The lighted Birthday Cake

Like the lighted Christmas tree, the lighted
birthday cake originated in medieval Germany, where
it was the centerpiece for the children's birthday
celebrations known as *Kinderfesten*, or "children's
festivals." The first birthday cakes were fruitcakes,
luxurious sweets made without leavening. The birthday
rituals of the gathering of family and friends,
the lighted candles, the birthday wish, the gift giving,
and the sharing of a sweet cake all began in pagan
rituals that were performed to drive away evil spirits and
court the favor of benevolent ones. In Germany,
the lighted cake was presented to the birthday child
when he or she awoke in the morning, and the candles
were kept lighted all day by replacing them as
needed. The cake was served, and the candles finally
blown out, after the evening meal.

Jelly Roll

◎

SOUTHERN COOKS HAVE ALWAYS PRIDED THEMSELVES ON THEIR BAKING,
AND ROBBIN GOURLEY'S FAMILY WAS NO EXCEPTION. HERE IS HER STORY OF THE
BIRTHDAY CAKE HER AUNT FLORENCE MADE EVERY YEAR, FROM ROBBIN'S BOOK
SUGAR PIE AND JELLY ROLL: SWEETS FROM A SOUTHERN KITCHEN.

*My mother, Pam, and I were always warmly welcomed into Aunt Florence's parlor while everyone else was accepted
under sufferance. Now I know why. She never accepted the rest of my mother's family, the Ireland clan.
Differing so greatly from the world where she grew up, the Irelands were boisterous, party-loving practical jokers.
She married my Uncle Teenan before she even knew the relations and advised me against
any future foolhardiness. She had met Teenan, fallen hopelessly in love, and married him after a short courtship.
He moved her from her beloved Baltimore to Alamance County in rural North Carolina and
built them a little house where they lived until he died. Then Aunt Florence sold the house (refusing to sell it to the
Irelands, though it adjoined their property), packed her bags, and hightailed it back to Baltimore.*

*Aunt Florence maintained, over the years, a silent and obsessive competition in baking with the Irelands.
Her most prized and famous dessert, jelly roll, showed up once a year at Mamaw's birthday.
It was meant to outdo her acquired relatives, and it always did.*

—ROBBIN GOURLEY

MAKES ONE 12-INCH JELLY ROLL; SERVES 8	3 eggs	1 cup sifted confectioners' sugar for
	½ cup granulated sugar	dredging
	½ cup all-purpose flour	1 cup jelly or jam, such as seedless
	½ teaspoon baking powder	raspberry jam or fig preserves
	¼ teaspoon salt	Fresh berries for garnish
	1 tablespoon hot water	Whipped cream for serving (page 95)

Place rack on the top position in the oven. Preheat the oven to 425°F. Line a 9-by-12-inch jelly roll pan with parchment paper.

In a large metal bowl, combine the eggs and sugar. Set the bowl over a pan of hot water and whisk until light, creamy, and thick enough to retain the impression of the whisk for a few seconds. Remove the bowl from heat and continue to whisk until cool.

Sift half of the flour with the baking powder and salt over the egg mixture. Using a rubber spatula, gently fold in the flour mixture. Add the remaining flour in the same way. Lightly stir in the hot water.

Pour the mixture into the prepared pan, spreading it evenly over the surface. Bake for 7 to 9 minutes, or until golden brown, well risen, and firm.

While the cake is baking, lay out a long sheet of waxed paper and liberally sprinkle it with the confectioners'

sugar. Place the paper over a tea towel that has been soaked in hot water and then lightly wrung out. In a small saucepan, gently warm the jelly or jam over low heat.

Turn the cake quickly out onto the paper, trim off the crusty edges with a sharp knife, and give them to a small child to nibble. Spread the cake with the warm jelly or jam. Roll the cake up with the edge of the paper, beginning with one long side and making the first turn firmly so that the cake will roll evenly and have a good shape when finished, but rolling more lightly after this first turn. Roll the cake to dredge it in the remaining confectioners' sugar. Transfer the cake to a wire cake rack and let it cool thoroughly.

Place the cake on a cake plate and surround it with fresh berries. Cut into 1-inch slices and serve, accompanied with a bowl of whipped cream.

German Chocolate Cake

JOHN MARTIN TAYLOR

JOHN MARTIN TAYLOR IS ONE OF A SMALL GROUP OF FOOD WRITERS DEDICATED TO PASSING ON RECIPES FOR REGIONAL SOUTHERN AND TRADITIONAL AMERICAN DISHES, FIRST IN HIS *HOPPIN' JOHN'S LOWCOUNTRY COOKING*, THEN IN *THE NEW SOUTHERN COOK*, FROM WHICH THIS RECIPE WAS TAKEN. GERMAN CHOCOLATE CAKE, WITH ITS TENDER TEXTURE, LIGHT CHOCOLATE FLAVOR, AND DELICIOUS COCONUT-PECAN FROSTING, IS AN AMERICAN CLASSIC THAT FIRST APPEARED IN THE 1950S, MADE WITH BAKER'S GERMAN'S SWEET CHOCOLATE. JOHN'S VERSION, A VARIATION ON THE ORIGINAL RECIPE, IS A GOOD BIRTHDAY CAKE FOR ALMOST ALL TEENAGERS AND ADULTS, INCLUDING THOSE WHO ARE NOT USUALLY CHOCOLATE-LOVERS.

MAKES ONE 9-INCH 3-LAYER CAKE; SERVES 12

4 ounces sweet or bittersweet chocolate
½ cup boiling water
4 large eggs, separated, at room temperature
1 cup (2 sticks) unsalted butter at room temperature
2 cups sugar
1 teaspoon baking soda
1 cup buttermilk at room temperature
2 cups unbleached all-purpose flour
½ teaspoon salt
1 teaspoon vanilla extract

ICING:
1 cup heavy cream
1 cup sugar
3 large egg yolks
½ cup (1 stick) unsalted butter
1 teaspoon vanilla extract
1¼ cups (6 ounces) fresh or frozen grated coconut (see note)
1 cup chopped pecans

MAKES 2¾ CUPS, ENOUGH TO FROST 1 CAKE

Preheat the oven to 350°F. Butter the bottoms and sides of three 9-inch round cake pans. Line the bottoms with rounds of parchment paper or waxed paper and butter the paper. Butter the sides again.

In a small bowl, combine the chocolate and boiling water and stir until melted. In a large bowl, beat the egg whites until they form soft peaks; set aside. Using the same whisk or beaters, cream the butter in a large bowl and gradually beat in the sugar. Add the egg yolks, one at a time, beating well after each addition. Add the chocolate mixture and beat until blended.

In a small bowl, combine the baking soda and buttermilk. Stir to blend. Sift the flour and salt together onto a piece of waxed paper. Add the dry ingredients to the batter in 3 increments, alternating with the buttermilk and ending with the flour. Stir in the vanilla.

With a large whisk, reach down into the beaten egg whites and make sure they're still whipped throughout. If not, beat them until they are. Pick up a large whiskful of the whites and mix into the batter to lighten it. Gently fold in the remaining whites.

Divide the batter among the prepared pans and smooth the tops with a rubber spatula. Bake for 30 minutes, or until a cake tester or wooden toothpick inserted in the center of the cakes comes out clean. Let cool in the pans on wire racks for 15 minutes, then unmold onto the racks and let cool completely.

Meanwhile, make the icing: In a saucepan, combine the cream, sugar, egg yolks, and butter. Place over medium heat and cook, stirring often, until the mixture is very thick, about 20 minutes. Remove from heat and stir in the vanilla. Fold in the coconut and nuts. Let cool completely.

To assemble, remove the paper from the layers. Place 1 layer right side up on a cake plate. Spread with one-third of the icing. Repeat with the remaining layers. Stack the layers. Do not ice the sides of the cake, but let the filling show through.

NOTE: Unsweetened coconut is sold frozen in 6-ounce packages as "flaked." Don't worry if the coconut isn't completely thawed when you stir it in. You'll have to stir in more vigorously to get it to break up evenly, but the icing will cool off more quickly.

1-2-3-4 Cake

Alice Waters, owner of the world-famous Chez Panisse restaurant in
Berkeley, California, is known as the mother of California cuisine.
This simple, traditional yellow cake is included in her children's cookbook,
Fanny at Chez Panisse, written for and with her daughter,
Fanny. The name of the recipe comes from the amounts for the ingredients,
which are so easy to remember that you don't have to write
them down. Simple enough for a child to make, it makes a lovely birthday
cake or cupcakes. Alice suggests filling the cake with
Lemon Curd (page 92) and decorating it with fresh violets.

Makes two
8- or 9-inch
cakes;
serves 8 to 10

1 cup (2 sticks) unsalted butter at
   room temperature
2 cups sugar
3 cups sifted cake flour
4 teaspoons baking powder

½ teaspoon salt
4 eggs, separated
1 teaspoon vanilla extract
1 cup milk

Turn on the oven to 350°F. Measure all the ingredients and get organized before you begin to make the batter. The butter should be soft. Cut it into small pieces, and put in a large bowl. Measure the sugar and set aside.

Sift the cake flour, scoop it into a measuring cup, scrape a knife across the top of the cup to level it, and measure 3 cups. Put the flour in a separate bowl. Measure level teaspoons of the baking powder and add to the flour. Measure the salt and add to the flour. Mix together.

Separate the eggs. Put the whites in one bowl and the yolks in another. Have the vanilla ready, and measure the milk and set aside.

Butter the insides of two 8- or 9-inch cake pans. Rub a small amount of butter all over the inside; don't miss the corners. Then put a tablespoon or so of flour in the pan and turn it all around so the pan is completely dusted with flour. Turn the pan upside down, and tap the edge on the table to let the extra flour fall out.

Now everything is ready to make the batter. Beat the butter with a wooden spoon or an electric mixer until light and fluffy. Add the sugar and beat again until very fluffy and light yellow. This is what it means to *cream* the butter and sugar. Add the egg yolks and beat them in briefly. Add 1 teaspoon vanilla and mix it in well.

Next add the flour and milk in parts. Sift about half of the flour over the butter mixture and lightly stir it in. Exchange the spoon for a large rubber spatula, and pour in about half the milk. Use the spatula to gently mix the milk into the batter. Sift over the rest of the flour and stir it in. Pour in the rest of the milk and gently mix it in.

The last step is to beat the egg whites and fold them into the batter. Put the egg whites in a very clean metal bowl, and beat with a whisk or mixer. They will gradually thicken and get very white as you beat in air bubbles. When the whites are very fluffy and will hold a soft peak shape when you lift up the whisk, they're ready.

CONTINUED

Scoop up some of the whites with the spatula, add it to the batter, and very gently stir them in. This will lighten the batter and make it easier to fold in the rest of the whites. Then pour the rest of the whites onto the batter and begin to fold them in. Folding is more delicate than stirring. Use the spatula to lift up some of the batter from the bottom of the bowl and fold it over the egg whites. Turn the bowl a little and fold again. Do that just until the egg whites are mixed in. The air bubbles in the whites will give the cake a light and delicate texture.

Divide the batter between the cake pans, and put in the center of the oven to bake for about 25 minutes. When the cakes are lightly browned, and a toothpick stuck in the center comes out clean, they're done. Remove from the oven and cool on a rack.

Note: You can cut the recipe in half to make a single layer cake.

1-2-3-4 Cupcakes: Butter 32 standard muffin cups or line them with paper liners. Fill each cup half full with batter. Bake in a preheated 350°F oven for about 25 minutes, or until a tester inserted in the center of a cupcake comes out clean. Frost with Buttercream Frosting (page 98). Makes 32 cupcakes.

Our Variation: For taller cupcakes, fill 24 standard muffin cups three-fourths full.

Party Themes and Favors

Planning a birthday party around a specific theme
is a delightful way to inspire creative cake decorating
and memorable party favors:

Plastic insects and candy worms are fun for children and a
good way to encourage their interest in the natural world.
Decorate a cake or cupcakes with little plastic insects
and a real vine (page 51). Give little prize cups to the guests
filled with edible candy worms and insects.

Decorate a cake or cupcakes for a bird-lover with little
tin bird pins (page 123), or look for ceramic or
plastic bird cake toppers at cake supply stores or children's
toy and nature stores.

A princess cake decorated with a fresh rose (page 69)
is charming for a sixteenth birthday, while younger girls will
love a doll princess cake (page 72) and a chance for her and her
guests to dress up in plastic crowns or tiaras.

Grownup birthday girls might want to celebrate a
significant birthday with a queen party theme: See our chocolate
soufflé cake with a crown stenciled on the top (page 86).

Sheet cakes can be cut into the shapes of different
animals, like our Pink Elephant Cutout Cake, the centerpiece
for an all-pink party (see page 109).

Whatever the theme, please remember to protect your little
guests by removing any small plastic objects before serving.

Fastest Fudge Cake

ALICE MEDRICH, THE WOMAN WHO BROUGHT THE FRENCH CHOCOLATE
TRUFFLE TO AMERICA AT COCOLAT, HER BERKELEY STORE, WENT ON TO WRITE A SERIES
OF HIGHLY REGARDED BAKING BOOKS. THE RECIPE FOR THE CAKE ALICE,
AND HER DAUGHTER AND NIECES MAKE EACH YEAR FOR HER MOTHER'S BIRTHDAY IS TAKEN
FROM ONE OF THEM, *A YEAR IN CHOCOLATE*.

Six years ago my daughter, Lucy, then eight years old, met her two age-mate Russian cousins for the first time. Even without a common language, it was love at first sight. Later that year I recruited Lucy and her cousins (already speaking English nonstop) to frost and decorate my mom's birthday cake. Encrusted with at least an inch of sparkly multicolored sugar, chocolate jimmies, gold and silver shot, mini gumdrops, and gobs of extra frosting "squirted" on top with a pastry bag, that cake was thrilling to behold. Grandma was touched.

The following year I devised an especially simple cake recipe so that the girls could help mix and bake the cake as well as decorate it. They have continued to make Grandma's birthday cake ever since. Now they are young teenagers and, of course, quite sophisticated. The whole family has noticed that the cake is getting less gaudy over time. An elegant piped border and "Happy Birthday Grandma" written in tasteful chocolate script in the center of the cake have replaced heaping coils of extra frosting. A few silver dragées have edged out the colorful sugar crystals, and I haven't seen a gumdrop garnish for some time now. We're all looking forward to Grandma Bea's eightieth this year. Here is the recipe for her cake: delicious, simple, and perfect for girls of all ages.

—ALICE MEDRICH

MAKES ONE
8-INCH SQUARE
OR 9-INCH
ROUND CAKE;
SERVES 8 TO 10

1 cup all-purpose flour
¼ cup plus 2 tablespoons unsweetened
   natural cocoa powder
½ teaspoon baking soda
¼ teaspoon salt
½ cup (1 stick) unsalted butter, melted
   and warm
1¼ cups packed brown sugar
2 large eggs
1 teaspoon vanilla extract
½ cup hot water

FAST FUDGE FROSTING:

MAKES 1½ CUPS,
ENOUGH TO
FROST 1 CAKE

5 tablespoons unsalted butter
¾ cup granulated sugar
⅔ cup unsweetened cocoa powder
Pinch of salt
¾ cup heavy cream
1 teaspoon vanilla extract

Position a rack in the lower third of the oven. Preheat
the oven to 350°F. Butter the bottom of an 8-inch
square or 9-inch round cake pan, or line it with parchment paper or waxed paper.

In a medium bowl, combine the flour, cocoa, baking
soda, and salt. Whisk to blend. Sift only if the cocoa
remains lumpy. Set aside.

In a large bowl, combine the warm melted butter and
brown sugar. Add the eggs and vanilla and beat until
well blended. Add all of the flour mixture at once. Using
a rubber spatula or wooden spoon, stir just until all the
flour mixture is moistened. Pour the hot water over the
batter all at once. Stir just until the water is incorporated and the batter is smooth.

Scrape the batter into the prepared pan. Bake for 25
to 30 minutes, or until a cake tester or toothpick inserted in the center comes out clean. Transfer the pan to a
wire rack and let the cake cool for about 10 minutes. To
unmold, slide a slim knife around the edges of the cake
to release it from the pan. Invert the cake and peel off
the paper liner. Turn the cake right side up onto a wire
rack and let cool completely. Or, leave the cake in the
pan and frost only the top of the cake.

To make the frosting: In a medium saucepan, melt the
butter. Stir in the granulated sugar, cocoa, and salt.
Gradually stir in the cream. Heat, stirring constantly,
until the mixture is smooth and hot but not boiling.
Remove from the heat and stir in the vanilla. Let cool
until thickened to spreading consistency, or use warm
for a glaze or a sauce.

Frost the top and sides of the cake. Store any leftover
frosting in the refrigerator for up to 3 days. Rewarm
gently in a pan of barely simmering water or in a
microwave before using.

NOTE: Natural (rather than Dutch-processed) cocoa is
called for in the cake recipe because it reacts with the
baking soda to make the cake rise properly and delivers
a brighter, truer chocolate flavor.

Becky's Birthday Cake

Tasha Tudor is well known both for her beloved children's books and illustrations, and for the nineteenth-century lifestyle she maintains at Corgi Cottage in Vermont. The recipes in the *Tasha Tudor Cookbook* are simple and traditional as well, including this classic white cake she bakes for family birthdays. Her method of serving it is also classic Tasha Tudor.

This receipt has been the family birthday cake for as long as I can remember. For many of my daughter Bethany's birthday parties we placed the cake on a wood-shingle raft, surrounded it with flowers, and floated it down our stream. We also had a shingle raft and a candle for each child's sandwich. We positioned the guests downstream, and when the right moment came we would light the candles and send the cake and its flotilla of shingle boats out into the stream. It was dark by then, so you can imagine the surprise of the guests at the sudden appearance of this fairy convoy. Once, the cake took off into a faster current and my son Seth had to wade in to rescue it.... I traditionally ice this cake with Boiled White Frosting (receipt follows) tinted pink. —Tasha Tudor

MAKES ONE
8-INCH 2-LAYER
CAKE; SERVES
10 TO 12

1 farm-fresh large egg, separated, at
   room temperature
4 tablespoons unsalted butter at room
   temperature
¾ cup sugar
1½ cups cake flour, sifted
2 teaspoons baking powder
⅛ teaspoon salt
½ cup milk
½ teaspoon vanilla extract

MAKES 4 CUPS,
ENOUGH TO
FROST ONE
8- OR 9-INCH
2-LAYER CAKE
OR 24 CUPCAKES

BOILED WHITE FROSTING:
2 large farm-fresh egg whites at room
   temperature
1½ cups sugar
½ cup water
½ teaspoon vanilla extract

Preheat the oven to 350°F. Butter the sides and bottoms of two 8-inch round cake pans. Line the bottoms with rounds of parchment paper or waxed paper. Butter and flour the paper and the sides of the pans; knock out the excess flour.

In a small bowl, beat the egg yolk. In a large bowl, cream the butter and sugar together until light and fluffy. Beat in the egg yolk. Sift the sugar, cake flour, baking powder, and salt together onto a piece of waxed paper. Add the dry ingredients to the butter mixture, alternating with the milk. Mix well.

In a medium bowl, beat the egg white until stiff, glossy peaks form. Fold the egg white and vanilla into the batter.

Pour the batter into the prepared pans and smooth the tops with a rubber spatula. Bake for about 30 minutes, or until a cake tester or wooden toothpick inserted in the center of the cakes comes out clean. Take care not to overbake. Let the cakes cool in the pans on wire racks for 10 minutes. Unmold the cakes onto the racks, peel off the paper, and let cool completely.

To make the frosting: In a medium bowl, beat the egg whites until stiff, glossy peaks form. In a double boiler over barely simmering water, combine the sugar and water. Stir until the sugar is dissolved. Boil without stirring until the mixture spins a thread when blown from a spoon, 242°F on a candy thermometer. Gradually beat the syrup into the egg whites in a thin stream. Add the vanilla and continue beating until the mixture reaches spreading consistency. Remove from heat and let cool.

Fill and frost the cake with the boiled white frosting.

NOTE: You can tint the frosting a delicate shade of pink with a bit of maraschino cherry juice.

James Villas and
Martha Pearl Villas

Paw Paw's Birthday Caramel Cake with Caramel Frosting

In James Villas's wonderful book of recipes, *My Mother's Southern Desserts*, he writes about his mother's love of making birthday cakes: "Never is the Southern obsession with rich, dramatic desserts more obvious than when Mother goes to town over a birthday, and never (I'm convinced) does she enjoy baking more than for this most special of occasions." This is the cake she makes for her son's birthday.

Mercy, this cake is wonderful, and I can remember, as a child, looking forward to my grandfather Paw Paw's birthday only because I knew Mother would be making a big caramel cake for him and I'd be allowed to lick the frosting bowl and spoon. (She now makes it for my birthday.) The cake has been in our family at least four generations, and Mother has already handed down the recipe to my young niece. For me, this has always been the supreme birthday cake. Paw Paw had to have vanilla ice cream with his caramel cake; I like mine plain—and eaten with my fingers. —James Villas

Makes one
3-layer 9-inch
square cake;
serves 8 to 10

2⅔ cups all-purpose flour
2 teaspoons baking powder
1 teaspoon salt
1 cup (2 sticks) unsalted butter at room temperature
2 cups granulated sugar
4 eggs, separated
1 cup milk
1 teaspoon vanilla extract

Caramel Frosting:
½ cup (1 stick) unsalted butter
1½ cups firmly packed dark brown sugar
½ cup milk
4 cups confectioners' sugar, sifted

Makes 3 cups,
enough to
frost 1 cake

Preheat the oven to 350°F. Butter and flour three 9-inch square baking pans; tap out any excess flour and set aside.

In a medium bowl, combine the flour, baking powder, and salt, and mix well. In a large bowl, beat the butter and sugar together until light and fluffy, then beat in the egg yolks, one at a time. Alternately add the dry ingredients and milk to the batter, beginning and ending with the dry ingredients.

In another large bowl, beat the egg whites until stiff, glossy peaks form, then gently fold them into the batter. Stir in the vanilla. Scrape the batter into the prepared pans and bake for 20 to 30 minutes, or until a cake tester inserted in the center of each layer comes out clean. Let cool completely in the pans.

To make the frosting: In a large, heavy saucepan, melt the butter over low heat. Add the brown sugar and milk and, stirring, bring the mixture to a boil. Remove from the heat and let cool. Gradually stir in the confectioners' sugar until well blended and very smooth.

Run a knife around the edges of each cake layer and unmold onto wire racks. Stack the layers on top of each other and spread the frosting over the top of each layer, then all around the sides, with a knife.

Ring Dropping

In the coastal southern states of the Carolinas, where I was born and reared, we had a lovely birthday custom of "ring dropping." When the person who was "yearing" (as they say in that part of the country) was presented with a cake full of lighted candles, all the guests crowded round to choose one of the outside candles. One by one, each person dropped his or her ring over a candle; some chose the same one, so that often the rings would be stacked high. How far your ring sank into the Chantilly cream, grated coconut, or chocolate mousse depended largely on whether you were wearing a handsome faceted stone or a heavy insignia ring.

Everyone then made a wish, along with the birthday person, and hoped, with folded hands and often with closed eyes, that the ring-laden candle would go out with the mighty blow that now had become an obligation. More often than not, that vigorous puff brought everyone's wish safely home.

Before the cake was cut, you claimed your ring, along with your own portion of the icing it invariably picked up.

—Patricia Kislevitz

Grandmothers' Chocolate Cake

THIS RECIPE, FROM CELEBRATED PASTRY CHEF EMILY LUCHETTI'S BOOK
STARS DESSERTS, COMBINES TWO FAMILY TRADITIONS AND MAKES A GLORIOUSLY TALL
BIRTHDAY CAKE WITH A LUSCIOUS DARK CHOCOLATE FROSTING.

*One of the high points of growing up with a twin brother was that on our birthday we always got two cakes!
My mom felt it was important that we each get our own and not have to share. We conspired
together to choose our flavors, making sure to never ask for the same kind. Every year one of our selections was
always chocolate cake with chocolate frosting. I even have the cake plate my mom used to serve
the cake on. Every time I see it, it makes me think of blowing out candles and sharing my birthday with my brother.*

*Years later when I met my husband, I found out that his family had a great recipe for a
chocolate cake his grandmother used to make. I combined her cake recipe with my grandmother's chocolate frosting
and created a recipe that we are now taking into the next generation.*

—EMILY LUCHETTI

MAKES ONE
8-INCH 3-LAYER
CAKE;
SERVES 10 TO 12

- 1½ cups plus 1 tablespoon unsweet- ened cocoa powder
- 1¼ cups boiling water
- 1½ cups cake flour
- 1½ cups plus 2 tablespoons all-purpose flour
- 1¼ teaspoons baking powder
- 1¼ teaspoons baking soda
- 10 tablespoons (1¼ sticks) unsalted butter at room temperature
- 2¾ cups firmly packed brown sugar
- 3 large eggs
- 1¼ cups buttermilk
- 1¼ teaspoons vanilla extract

BITTERSWEET CHOCOLATE
FROSTING:
- 4 ounces bittersweet chocolate, chopped
- 8 ounces unsweetened chocolate, chopped
- 1 cup (2 sticks) unsalted butter
- 3 cups confectioners' sugar
- Pinch of salt
- 2 teaspoons vanilla extract
- ¾ cup plus 2 tablespoons milk

MAKES 3 CUPS,
ENOUGH TO
FROST 1 CAKE

Preheat the oven to 350°F. Butter three 8-inch round cake pans.

In a small bowl, whisk the cocoa and boiling water together, making a smooth paste. Set aside to cool. Sift the cake flour, all-purpose flour, baking powder, and bak- ing soda together onto a sheet of waxed paper.

Put the butter and brown sugar in the bowl of a heavy- duty electric mixer fitted with the paddle attachment. Cream on medium-high speed for 2 minutes, or until light and fluffy. Add the eggs, one at time, beating well after each addition. Decrease the speed to low and add the dry ingredients alternately with the buttermilk. Mix in the vanilla and the cocoa paste.

Divide the batter evenly among the prepared pans. Bake the layers for about 25 minutes, or until a skewer inserted in the center of a cake comes out clean. Transfer the cakes to wire racks and let cool completely. Unmold them by running a knife along the inside edge of each pan and inverting them.

To make the frosting: In a double boiler over simmering water, melt the chocolates and butter together. Remove from heat and let cool to lukewarm.

Sift the confectioners' sugar and salt together into a large bowl. In a small bowl, combine the vanilla and the milk. Whisk the milk mixture into the confectioners' sugar. Add the melted chocolate mixture and stir until smooth. Fill and frost the cake with the frosting.

Benoît's Upside-Down Caramelized Apple Tart

FOOD WRITER PATRICIA WELLS HAS LIVED IN FRANCE FOR SOME TWENTY YEARS NOW,
TURNING OUT INVALUABLE GUIDES TO THE FOOD OF HER ADOPTED COUNTRY,
SUCH AS *FOOD LOVER'S GUIDE TO FRANCE* AND *THE PARIS COOKBOOK*, FROM WHICH
THIS CLASSIC RECIPE FOR TARTE TATIN BY BENOÎT GUICHARD IS TAKEN.

*Each year in France high achievers in all of the nation's trades—from hairdressers to chefs to florists—
compete for the top honor of Meilleur Ouvrier de France. When chef Benoît Guichard of Jamin competed, he
placed first in the pastry category, outdistancing famous pastry chefs vying for the title.
Come autumn, I make this tart every single chance I get. I love it so much that I make it for my birthday in November,
in lieu of a cake! Note that the apples cook on top of the stove for one full hour before baking.
This seems like a long time, but your palate will be rewarded!* —PATRICIA WELLS

MAKES ONE
9-INCH TART;
SERVES 8

FLAKY PASTRY:
1 cup unbleached all-purpose flour
⅛ teaspoon fine sea salt
½ cup (1 stick) cold unsalted butter,
   cut into cubes
3 tablespoons ice water

¾ cup sugar
10 tablespoons unsalted butter, cut
   into thin slices
1 teaspoon vanilla extract
3 pounds large apples (about 8),
   peeled, cored, and halved lengthwise
   (see note)
Crème fraîche or whipped heavy cream
   for garnish

To make the pastry: In a food processor, combine the flour and salt. Process to blend. Add the butter and process until well blended, about 10 seconds. With the machine running, add the ice water and process just until the mixture begins to form a ball, about 10 seconds.

Transfer the dough to a clean work surface and, with a dough scraper or the heel of your hand, smear it bit by bit across the work surface until it is smooth and the flour and butter are well blended. Form into a flattened round, wrap in plastic wrap, and refrigerate for at least 1 hour or up to 24 hours.

On a lightly floured board, roll the dough out into a 10-inch round. Place it on a piece of parchment paper or waxed paper. Refrigerate for at least 1 hour or up to 24 hours.

Spread the sugar evenly over the bottom of a 9-inch tarte Tatin pan or heavy ovenproof skillet. Place the butter slices evenly over the sugar. Drizzle with the vanilla extract.

Beginning at the edge of the pan, stand the apple halves on end on top of the butter: They should all face in one direction, with the rounded edge of the apple against the edge of the pan and the cut side toward the center. Pack the apples as close together as possible. Make a second circle of apple halves inside the first. Place one apple half in the center of the circle to fill any remaining space. (As they cook, the apples will shrink and give up their juices. They will also naturally fall into place as they shrink, with the rounded halves falling to the bottom.) CONTINUED

Place the pan over low heat and cook the apples in the butter and sugar, uncovered, until the butter mixture turns a thick, golden brown, about 1 hour. The liquid should remain at a gentle bubble. Baste the apples from time to time to speed up the cooking and evenly cook the fruit. (If the apples lose their place, you can carefully nudge them back into formation.)

Preheat the oven to 425°F. Place the pan on a baking sheet lined with parchment paper. Remove the pastry from the refrigerator and place it on top of the apples, gently pushing the edges of the pastry down around the inside edge of the pan. Place in the oven and bake until the pastry is golden, 25 to 30 minutes. Do not be concerned if the juices bubble over—this is normal.

Remove the tart from the oven. Immediately invert a rimmed serving platter over the tart pan. Quickly but carefully invert the tart pan and the platter together so the pastry ends up on the platter, with the apples on top. Should any apples stick to the bottom of the pan, remove them and place them back in the tart. Serve warm or at room temperature, with dollops of crème fraîche or whipped cream.

NOTE: Recommended varieties of apples for a tarte Tatin: Cox's Orange Pippin, Fuji, Criterion, Winesap, Northern Spy, Jonagold. Make this only in season, meaning when apples are at their peak in the early fall to late winter. If you use older, softer apples, they are likely to fall apart and turn into applesauce.

Treasure Strings

The games children traditionally play at birthday
parties range from pin the tail on the donkey, drop the
handkerchief, and blindman's buff to musical chairs
and treasure hunts. A variation on the treasure hunt that
younger children always seem to love is called
treasure strings: Choose a different color of a ball of
yarn for each child and tie a tag with the child's
name to the beginning of the yarn. Then, weave the
yarn through the house, over and under furniture, rugs,
and objects and crossing over and under the other
pieces of yarn. At the end of each piece, tie a small gift
and hide the gift under something. Each child follows his
or her piece to the end, and is rewarded with a
small treasure. The first child to find his or her gift
may also receive a prize.

Grandmother Whitehead's
Famous Texas Fudge Cake

THIS RECIPE FROM *THE CHICKEN SOUP FOR THE SOUL COOKBOOK*
IS FOR AN EASY-TO-MAKE LARGE CHOCOLATE SHEET CAKE. FOR A CAKE THAT WILL SERVE
24, MAKE 2 CAKES AND STACK THEM TO MAKE 2 LAYERS.

I come from a family of great cooks....
One of the best gatherings we have had in the
name of food was my brother's
twenty-sixth birthday. For me, it changed
forever the meaning of the annual
celebration; it was The Best Birthday.

All in the family gathered at my sister's
beautiful Southwestern-style home
in northern California for an evening of
gourmet food and birthday cake ...
as we all reached for seconds, we suddenly
realized that this meal, no matter
how exquisite, was not going to be complete
without hearing from the birthday boy.

Bob started to give a little speech,
then said, "I feel like I am pretty confused at
this age. What I'd really like
to hear is what each of you were doing
when you were twenty-six."

... One by one, we spoke. We celebrated birth,
confusion, change and loss as the wheel
of my brother's life turned. Another birthday,
the passing of yet another year.

And yes, we ate the famous
Texas Fudge Cake, since it is my
brother's favorite. It tasted especially
wonderful that night.

—MARY OLSEN KELLY

MAKES ONE
11-BY-15-INCH
CAKE; SERVES
ABOUT 12

⅓ cup unsweetened cocoa powder
1 cup water
1 cup (2 sticks) unsalted butter
2 cups all-purpose flour
2 cups granulated sugar
1 teaspoon baking soda
½ teaspoon salt
2 large eggs, lightly beaten
½ cup sour cream or buttermilk (sour
    cream is richer)
1 teaspoon vanilla extract

MAKES 2 CUPS,
ENOUGH TO
FROST 1 CAKE

ICING:
6 tablespoons unsalted butter
¼ cup milk
3 tablespoons unsweetened cocoa
    powder
3 cups confectioners' sugar
¾ cup finely chopped nuts of your
    choice
1 teaspoon vanilla extract

Preheat the oven to 350°F. Butter an 11-by-15-inch pan.

Put the cocoa in a medium saucepan and gradually stir in the water. Bring to a boil, add the butter, and let melt. Remove from the heat and set aside.

Sift the flour, sugar, baking soda, and salt together onto a piece of waxed paper. Gradually stir the dry ingredients into the cocoa mixture. Add the eggs, sour cream or buttermilk, and vanilla to the cocoa mixture and stir until smooth.

Pour the batter into the prepared pan. Bake for 30 minutes, or until the cake is firm to the touch in the center.

While the cake is baking, make the icing: In a medium saucepan, combine the butter, milk and cocoa. Bring to a boil and stir to melt the butter. Add the confectioners' sugar and beat until smooth. Stir in the nuts and vanilla.

Spread the icing over the *hot* cake (still in the pan). Let cool before cutting.

OUR VARIATION: Add 1 teaspoon ground cinnamon to the dry ingredients for a lightly spicy flavor.

Princess Cake

THE ELABORATELY DECORATED PRINCESS CAKE IS TRADITIONAL IN SWEDEN FOR A GIRL'S
SIXTEENTH BIRTHDAY. BECAUSE IT IS A COMPLEX CAKE WITH SEVERAL
DIFFERENT COMPONENTS, THE PRINCESS CAKE IS A BAKERY SPECIALTY, BUT THE
ADVENTUROUS HOME BAKER CAN MAKE ONE BY FOLLOWING THIS RECIPE FROM
GAYLE AND JOE ORTIZ'S *THE VILLAGE BAKER'S WIFE*. IT IS MADE WITH A BASIC GÉNOISE,
A FRENCH BUTTER SPONGE CAKE. GAYLE POINTS OUT THAT ALTHOUGH THIS
CAKE HAS MANY STEPS, ALL OF THE COMPONENTS CAN BE MADE AHEAD OF TIME AND
THE CAKE ASSEMBLED ON THE DAY OF THE CELEBRATION.

PRINCESS CAKE PREPARATION TIMELINE:
- Marzipan: One day to 1 month ahead
- Soaking Solution: One day to 1 month ahead
- Vanilla Genoise Layer Cake: One day ahead (refrigerate)
  or up to 1 week ahead (freeze)
- Pastry Cream: One to 3 days ahead
- Flavored Whipped Cream: Just before assembly

MAKES ONE
9-INCH 3-LAYER
CAKE; SERVES 12

VANILLA GENOISE LAYER CAKE:
5 large eggs
¾ cup granulated sugar
2 tablespoons unsalted butter
1 teaspoon vanilla extract
1 cup cake flour, sifted

Soaking Solution (recipe follows)
⅓ cup raspberry jam
1 cup Pastry Cream (recipe follows)
Marzipan at room temperature (recipe
  follows), see note

FLAVORED WHIPPED CREAM:
3 cups heavy cream
3 tablespoons granulated sugar
1 tablespoon vanilla extract

Confectioners' sugar for dusting
1 fresh pink or white rose for decorating (see page 24)

To make the cake: Preheat the oven to 350°F. Butter and flour one 9-by-2-inch cake pan or two 9-by-1½-inch cake pans; knock out the excess flour. Line the bottom of the pan(s) with a round of parchment paper. Fill a medium saucepan half full of water and bring to a boil.

Using a hand whisk, beat the eggs until blended in the bowl of a heavy-duty mixer. Whisk in the sugar. Place the bowl over the saucepan of boiling water. (The water should be at least 2 inches below the bottom of the bowl.) To prevent the eggs from cooking, use your hand to stir the mixture constantly until it feels quite warm. The eggs should remain liquid and not become opaque or cooked. (Failing to mix constantly will result in very sweet scrambled eggs!) Immediately remove the bowl from the heat,

fit the mixer with the whisk attachment, and start whipping the eggs on high speed without stopping for 3½ to 4 minutes.

Meanwhile, melt the butter and pour it into a small bowl. Add the vanilla. Place the flour in a sifter and set aside.

The egg mixture is ready when the eggs have just cooled and at least tripled in volume. When you lift the whisk out of the bowl, the batter should fall off the whisk in ribbons.

Remove the bowl from the mixer and sift a little less than one-fourth (a scant ¼ cup) of the flour over the surface of the batter. Using a rubber spatula, gently fold in the flour. Repeat until all the flour is incorporated.

Pour a generous cup of the batter over the melted butter mixture in the small bowl. Thoroughly fold the batter into

CONTINUED

the butter. Slowly pour the butter mixture over the remaining batter in the bowl in a circular motion. (If you add the butter mixture too quickly it will sink, reducing the volume and toughening the cake.) Gently fold together until none of the darker butter mixture is visible.

Carefully pour the batter into the prepared 9-by-2-inch pan; it should be about two-thirds full. If using two 9-by-1½-inch pans, pour one-third of the batter into one pan and the remaining two-thirds into the other pan. Set the cake pan(s) on a baking sheet and immediately place on the center rack in the oven. If using a 9-by-2-inch pan, bake for about 30 minutes and wait to open the oven until the cake has baked at least 25 minutes, or it may fall. If using 2 pans, bake for about 20 minutes and wait to open the oven until the cakes have baked at least 15 minutes. The cake is done when it just starts to pull away from the sides of the pan. (The cake will not spring back when gently pressed, and a toothpick will not come out clean when it is ready.)

Remove the cakes from the oven and immediately run a metal icing spatula or knife around the inside of the pan(s) to loosen the cake. Let cool for 5 minutes, then unmold and let cool completely. The cakes may be stored, well wrapped, in the refrigerator for 1 day, or frozen for up to 1 week.

- For optimum moistness, this cake is best baked in a 9-by-2 inch cake pan, then cut into 3 layers.
- Genoise may be cut into layers as soon as it is cool. If the cake has been refrigerated, cut it as soon as you remove it from the refrigerator. If it has been frozen, let it thaw about 30 minutes, then cut. Always cut off the top layer first and place it cut side down.
- If you precut the cake layers well before icing the cake, keep them covered with plastic wrap. Vanilla genoise dries out very quickly when left unwrapped.

Marzipan
Makes about 2 pounds

3 cups sifted confectioners' sugar
1 pound almond paste
3 tablespoons light corn syrup
2 to 3 tablespoons water
⅛ to ¼ teaspoon green food coloring (traditional for the princess cake)

Put the confectioners' sugar in the bowl of a heavy-duty mixer fitted with the flat beater. With the mixer running on medium-low speed, add the almond paste about 1 teaspoon at a time. This will take about 5 minutes. The mixture will be crumbly. Scrape down the bowl and beater. Add the corn syrup and mix on low speed until incorporated. The mixture will still be crumbly. Again scrape down the bowl and beater.

In a small bowl, combine the water and food coloring. With the mixer on medium-low speed, add about half of the food coloring mixture and beat until incorporated. Continue gradually adding the food coloring until the marzipan just comes together and reaches the consistency of sugar cookie dough. It should be smooth but not crumbly or overly sticky.

If more color is desired, knead it in by hand after removing the marzipan from the mixer. (Remember it is easier to add a little more color at the end than to make a new batch!) Different colors have different intensities and will require different amounts.

Place the marzipan on a sheet of plastic wrap and form it into a 9-inch disk about ½ inch thick. Wrap and refrigerate overnight before using. Store in an airtight container or covered in plastic wrap in the refrigerator for up to 1 month.

SOAKING SOLUTION
Makes about ¾ cup

½ cup water
¼ cup sugar
1 teaspoon Myers's dark rum

In a small saucepan, combine the water and sugar and bring just to a boil over medium heat. Remove from heat and let cool. Add the rum. Let cool completely before using or refrigerating. Store in an airtight container in the refrigerator for up to 1 month.

PASTRY CREAM
Makes 3 cups

1½ cups half-and-half
6 tablespoons cornstarch
½ cup sugar
½ cup water
4 large egg yolks at room temperature
1 teaspoon vanilla extract

In a heavy saucepan, warm the half-and-half over medium heat until it begins to simmer. Meanwhile, in a medium bowl, mix the cornstarch with the sugar. Using a whisk, whip in the water until smooth. Beat in the egg yolks. When the half-and-half is simmering, slowly add about half of it to the cornstarch mixture, whisking constantly to incorporate. Whisk this mixture into the simmering half-and-half and continue to whisk vigorously and constantly until the pastry cream thickens, 2 to 5 minutes.

Remove from heat, add the vanilla, and transfer to a glass or metal bowl. Let cool completely, stirring frequently to prevent a skin from forming on the top. Cover and refrigerate for at least 5 hours or up to 3 days.

TO ASSEMBLE THE PRINCESS CAKE:
When you are ready to assemble the cake, make the whipped cream: In a deep bowl, combine all the ingredients. Using an electric mixer or a balloon whisk, beat the mixture until soft peaks form. Set aside while cutting the cake.

Using a long, serrated knife, level the top(s) of the cakes. If you used a 9-by-2-inch pan, cut the cake into 3 even layers; if you used two 9-by-1½-inch pans, cut the thicker layer into 2 even layers. Place the top layer of the cake, cut side down, on a 9-inch cake cardboard. Brush it lightly with soaking solution, being careful not to over-soak it. Spread the cake with a thin layer of the raspberry jam. (You should almost be able to see through it.) Spread a ¼-inch-thick layer of the whipped cream over the raspberry jam. Set the middle layer of the cake on the whipped cream. Brush it with soaking solution and then spread it with a ⅜-inch-thick layer of pastry cream. Place the remaining cake layer, cut side down, on top of the pastry cream. Brush it with soaking solution.

Using a metal icing spatula, coat the side of the cake with a ⅛-inch-thick coat of whipped cream. There should be just enough whipped cream to seal in all the crumbs and to prevent the marzipan from resting directly on the cake.

Mound all the remaining whipped cream on the top of the cake and, using a metal icing spatula, spread into a dome so that the cake almost looks like an upside-down bowl. Soften the edge where the top of the genoise ends and the dome begins by beveling it with the flat part of the spatula.

CONTINUED

Bring the marzipan to room temperature at least 1 hour before assembling the cake. Before attempting to cover a cake with marzipan for the first time, practice covering an inverted 8- or 9-inch bowl. Once you are comfortable with this technique, gather up the marzipan, knead it into a ball, and reroll to cover the cake.

Lightly dust the work surface with confectioners' sugar. Place the marzipan on the surface and, using an 18-inch-wide rolling pin, roll out the marzipan as you would pie dough into a 16-inch circle, ⅛ inch thick. Frequently dust the marzipan with plenty of confectioners' sugar and turn the circle to make sure the marzipan is not sticking to the work surface. Using your hand, brush off the excess confectioners' sugar. Don't worry if a lot of confectioners' sugar clings to the marzipan; it will be absorbed.

Set the cake near the rolled-out marzipan about 6 inches away from the edge of the work surface so that you can see and reach around the entire cake. Loosely roll the marzipan onto the rolling pin, starting at the back and rolling toward you.

Lift the rolling pin with the marzipan rolled around it. Unroll the marzipan over the cake, starting at the front and unrolling toward the back, while making sure to cover the entire cake and cardboard. When finished, some marzipan should drape onto the work surface all around the cake.

At this point, the dome of the cake will be smoothly covered, but there will be folds or creases on the sides. To remove the folds or creases, lift the outside edge of the marzipan with a hand on either side of a fold and, without tearing or stretching, gently pull the marzipan out and down until the fold disappears.

Work your way around the cake. Once all the folds are eliminated, rub the palm of your hand around the sides of the cake to further smooth it and eliminate air pockets.

With a rolling pizza cutter or small, sharp knife, carefully cut off the excess marzipan along the bottom edge of the cake cardboard. (The cardboard should not show.) Reserve for making leaves.

Slide the icing spatula under the cake cardboard and tilt the cake up enough to get the palm of your other hand underneath to lift it without touching the sides. Turn the cake, checking to make sure the cake and cardboard are completely covered with the marzipan. If not, gently push the marzipan down, using the palm of your other hand.

Set the cake down and sift a fine dusting of confectioners' sugar over it. Transfer to a serving platter.

Cut 3 elongated ovals about 3 inches long by 1 inch wide out of the remaining marzipan to make 3 leaf shapes. Lightly score the top of the leaves with a knife to create veins. Gently bend each leaf into a leaflike curve. Place the marzipan leaves, spaced evenly apart, on the center of the domed cake top with the stem ends touching. Gently press the stem ends into the dome to secure the leaves to the top of the cake.

Cut the rose stem 2 inches below the flower. Lift the sepals so they will set over the marzipan leaves and insert the rose into the center of the dome.

The finished princess cake may be stored in the refrigerator for up to 2 days, but it is best the day it is made. Remove the cake from the refrigerator 30 minutes before serving.

Decorative Tip: To make the doll cake, purchase a "doll pick" from a cake-decorating store (see Resources, page 127).

BIRTHDAY CANDLES

The lighted candle has always resonated with the warmth,
fragility, and transcendent quality of human life.
The first known use of candles on cake dates back to
the Greeks, who placed honey cakes with lighted candles
on the altars of Artemis, the moon goddess—surely
because of their resemblance to the round, glowing moon.
Today, the lighted cake bears the freight of all
those meanings—even though we may not articulate
them—for the presentation of a birthday cake is always
an important and cherished gesture.

Old-Fashioned Banana Spice Cake

THIS LUXURIOUS CAKE, MADE WITH MASHED RIPE BANANAS AND FILLED WITH CREAMY CUSTARD AND SLICED BANANAS, IS FROM CELEBRATED CALIFORNIA CHEF, RESTAURATEUR, AND COOKBOOK AUTHOR BRADLEY OGDEN. THIS WAS ONE OF HIS FAVORITE BIRTHDAY CAKES WHILE HE WAS GROWING UP IN A FAMILY OF SEVEN CHILDREN. BRADLEY'S FATHER ALWAYS HELPED BAKE THE FAMILY BIRTHDAY CAKES, AND IT WAS HE WHO FIRST GAVE BRADLEY THE IDEA OF BECOMING A CHEF.

MAKES ONE
8-INCH 4-LAYER
CAKE; SERVES
10 TO 12

½ cup (1 stick) unsalted butter at room temperature
1½ cups granulated sugar
2 large eggs
1 cup mashed ripe banana (2 to 3 bananas)
1 teaspoon vanilla extract
2 cups cake flour
1 teaspoon baking soda
½ teaspoon salt
½ teaspoon ground cinnamon
⅛ teaspoon ground allspice
Pinch of ground mace
½ cup buttermilk at room temperature

FILLING:
¾ cup milk
¼ cup granulated sugar
2 large egg yolks
3 tablespoons flour
Pinch of salt
1 tablespoon unsalted butter
¾ teaspoon vanilla extract
1 or 2 tablespoons heavy cream (optional)
2 bananas, peeled and sliced

TOPPING:
1 cup heavy cream
3 tablespoons confectioners' sugar, sifted
¼ teaspoon vanilla extract

Preheat the oven to 350°F. Butter and lightly flour the sides and bottoms of two 8-inch round cake pans; knock out the excess flour.

Using an electric mixer on medium speed, cream the butter and sugar together in a large bowl for at least 10 minutes, or until very light and fluffy. Beat in the eggs, mashed banana, and vanilla. Sift the flour, baking soda, salt, and spices together onto a piece of waxed paper. Stir into the banana mixture alternately with the buttermilk.

Spoon into the prepared pans and smooth the tops with a rubber spatula. Bake for 25 to 30 minutes, or until a cake tester or wooden toothpick inserted in the center comes out clean. Transfer the pans to wire racks and let cool for 10 minutes. Unmold onto the racks and let cool completely.

While the cake bakes, make the filling: In a small, heavy saucepan, heat the milk until small bubbles form around the edges of the pan. Meanwhile, beat the sugar and egg yolks together in a small bowl. Beat in the flour and salt. Gradually beat in the hot milk.

Return to the saucepan and cook over medium heat, stirring constantly, until the mixture begins to thicken and comes to a simmer. Lower the heat to low and continue stirring for 2 minutes. Remove from heat and beat in the butter and vanilla. Pour into a bowl, cover with a piece of plastic wrap pressed onto the surface of the custard, let cool slightly, and refrigerate.

To assemble the cake: Split each cake layer in half. If the custard is too thick to spread, thin it with a little cream. Spread one-third of the filling and arrange one-third of the banana slices evenly on 3 of the layers. Stack the layers and top with the fourth layer. Cover with plastic wrap and refrigerate for 2 to 3 hours.

Just before serving, make the topping: In a deep bowl, whip the cream until very soft peaks form. Beat in the sugar and vanilla. Spread the whipped cream frosting over the top of the cake, allowing some to drip down the sides.

Le Kilimanjaro—
Glace au Chocolat, Pralinée

A DRAMATIC ICE CREAM CAKE FROM JULIA CHILD, AMERICA'S BELOVED "FRENCH CHEF,"
WHO SERVED IT FOR HER HUSBAND'S BIRTHDAY WHEN THEY WERE
ENSCONCED AT LA PITCHOUNE, THEIR HOUSE IN THE SOUTH OF FRANCE IN THE 1960S.
THE ICE CREAM MIXTURE IS FROZEN IN A MOLD, SO YOU DON'T NEED
AN ICE CREAM MAKER TO MAKE THIS UNCONVENTIONAL, SOPHISTICATED "CAKE."

*Only Sybille and Eda were invited for Paul's
birthday feast, which included
a flaming mountain of ice cream cake.
It was* Le Kilimanjaro, *the chocolate and
almond ice cream dessert,
which would appear in the second volume
of* Mastering *(page 420).
She added a touch that is not in the book:
on the top of the dessert
"mountain," she placed an empty half
eggshell, filled it with liquor,
and lighted it before taking the flaming
volcano to the table.*

—NOËL RILEY FITCH, FROM
*APPETITE FOR LIFE: THE
BIOGRAPHY OF JULIA CHILD*

TOASTED ALMOND BRITTLE
(*PRALIN AUX AMANDES*):
1 cup (4 ounces) blanched almonds
½ cup granulated sugar
3 tablespoons water

CHOCOLATE ICE CREAM
(*GLACE AU CHOCOLAT*):
½ cup granulated sugar
⅓ cup water
2 tablespoons instant coffee
6 ounces semisweet chocolate,
    chopped
2 ounces unsweetened chocolate,
    chopped
2 cups heavy cream
¾ cup plus 1 tablespoon toasted
    almond brittle, above

1 cup heavy cream
Confectioners' sugar to taste
½ teaspoon vanilla extract

To make the almond brittle: Preheat the oven to 350°F. Oil a roasting pan. Spread the almonds in a sided baking sheet and toast, stirring several times, for 10 to 15 minutes, or until a walnut brown. Remove from the oven.

In a small, heavy saucepan, combine the sugar and water. Set over medium-high heat. Swirl the pan slowly by its handle, but do not stir the sugar with a spoon while the liquid is coming to a boil. Continue swirling for a moment while the liquid boils and changes from cloudy to perfectly clear. Cover the pan, raise heat to high, and boil for several minutes until the bubbles are thick and heavy. Uncover, and continue boiling, swirling gently, until the syrup turns a nice caramel brown. Remove from heat and stir in the almonds; immediately turn out in the oiled pan. When cold and hard, after 20 minutes or so, break up. Grind ½ cup at a time in a blender.

To make the ice cream: In a medium saucepan, combine the sugar and water. Swirl over medium-high heat until the sugar has dissolved completely and the liquid is perfectly clear. Remove from heat; stir in the coffee. Stir in the chocolate, cover, and set the pan in a larger saucepan of simmering water removed from heat.

While the chocolate is melting, beat the cream: Pour the cream in a deep bowl and set it in a bowl of ice cubes and water. Beat until the cream has doubled in volume and the beater leaves light traces on the surface.

With an electric mixer, whip the chocolate until perfectly smooth and shiny. Beat the chocolate for a moment over ice to cool it, then beat in about ½ cup of the whipped cream. Finally, fold the chocolate mixture into the remaining whipped cream along with the almond brittle.

Immediately turn the ice cream mixture into a 6-cup conical mold or a narrow bowl with a rounded bottom, to give the effect of a mountain peak. Cover with plastic wrap and freeze for about 4 hours.

Just before serving, whip the 1 cup heavy cream, following the same method as used to whip the cream for the ice cream mixture. Beat in the confectioners' sugar and vanilla. Set aside.

Dip the bottom of the mold or bowl into tepid water to loosen the ice cream. Turn a serving dish upside down over the mold and reverse the two to unmold the cream onto the dish. Top with the whipped cream and sprinkle with the remaining almond brittle.

OUR NOTE: To make a flaming volcano cake like the one Julia made for Paul, fill an empty half eggshell with brandy, insert the eggshell into the summit of the cake, and light the brandy with a long-handled match. Serve immediately.

Meyer Lemon Pound Cake

STEPHANIE GREENLEIGH

ONE OF FOOD STYLIST STEPHANIE GREENLEIGH'S FAVORITE RECIPES, ORIGINALLY
PRINTED IN HER BOOK *BAKED FROM THE HEART*, THIS LEMON CAKE
MAKES A SOPHISTICATED, ELEGANT, AND FEMININE BIRTHDAY CAKE, ESPECIALLY
WHEN DUSTED WITH CONFECTIONERS' SUGAR AND DECORATED
WITH GLAZED FLOWERS (SEE PAGE 25) AND LONG FRENCH BIRTHDAY CANDLES.

MAKES ONE
6-CUP
BUNDT CAKE;
SERVES 12

2 cups cake flour
½ teaspoon cream of tartar
¼ teaspoon baking soda
¼ teaspoon salt
1 cup (2 sticks) unsalted butter at
  room temperature
1½ cups granulated sugar
5 large eggs at room temperature
1 teaspoon vanilla extract
1 tablespoon grated lemon zest

MEYER LEMON SYRUP:
½ cup fresh Meyer lemon juice
  (see note)
½ cup steeped herbal lemon tea
1 cup granulated sugar

Confectioners' sugar for dusting

Preheat the oven to 325°F. Brush a 6-cup Bundt cake pan
(of any shape) with butter and dust it with flour; knock
out the excess flour.

Sift the flour, cream of tartar, baking soda, and salt
together onto a piece of waxed paper.

In a large bowl, using an electric mixer on medium speed,
cream the butter and granulated sugar together until light
and fluffy. Beat in the eggs, one at a time, beating well
after each addition. Beat in the vanilla extract and lemon
zest. On low speed, gradually beat in the dry ingredients
just until blended. The batter will be stiff.

Pour the batter into the prepared pan and bake for 40
to 50 minutes, or until a toothpick inserted in the center
of the cake comes out clean.

Meanwhile, make the syrup: Combine all the ingredients in a small saucepan. Bring to a boil and cook for
about 5 minutes, or until the syrup thickens. Remove
from heat and let the syrup cool.

Transfer the pan to a wire rack and let cool for 10 minutes. Pierce the top of the cake all over with a toothpick to
help it absorb the syrup, and gradually pour the syrup
over the cake and down the sides. Let the cake cool in the

pan for 10 more minutes, then unmold onto the wire rack
and let cool completely. Dust with confectioners' sugar to
serve.

OUR NOTE: Meyer lemons are thin-skinned, plump fruits
with juice that is slightly less acidic than that of regular
lemons. If you can't find Meyer lemons, regular lemons
may be substituted.

Gold Cake with Grandma's Fudge Frosting

JIM FOBEL, A PROTÉGÉ OF JAMES BEARD, COUNTS AMONG HIS FAVORITE CAKES THIS CLASSIC GOLD CAKE WITH CHOCOLATE FROSTING. IT IS ALSO THE FIRST CAKE HE EVER BAKED, AS HE RECOUNTS BELOW. THIS RECIPE IS FROM *JIM FOBEL'S OLD-FASHIONED BAKING BOOK: RECIPES FROM AN AMERICAN CHILDHOOD.*

At the age of twelve I discovered for myself the magic of cake-baking when I decided to make a gold cake as a birthday surprise for my mother. I was so enthralled with the transformation of my newly mixed batter into cake that I stood on a chair to watch the entire proceeding through the window in the oven door. The project almost came to grief when I frosted the cake while it was still too warm and had to run to a neighbor for help as the layers slowly slid apart. Some toothpicks and a short spell in the refrigerator saved the day.

—JIM FOBEL

MAKES ONE
9-INCH 2-LAYER
CAKE; SERVES
10 TO 12

2½ cups sifted cake flour
4 teaspoons baking powder
¼ teaspoon salt
¾ cup (1½ sticks) unsalted butter at
    room temperature
1¼ cups sugar
8 egg yolks
1 teaspoon vanilla extract
¾ cup milk

MAKES 2½ CUPS,
ENOUGH TO
FROST 1 CAKE

GRANDMA'S FUDGE FROSTING:
1½ cups sugar
1 cup heavy cream
6 ounces unsweetened chocolate,
    chopped
½ cup (1 stick) unsalted butter, cut
    into pieces
2 teaspoons vanilla extract

Place a rack in the center of the oven. Preheat the oven
to 350°F. Butter and flour two 9-inch round cake pans;
knock out the excess flour.

Sift the cake flour, baking powder, and salt onto a
sheet of waxed paper.

In a large bowl, beat the butter until fluffy. Gradually
beat in the sugar and continue beating until blended.
Add the egg yolks and vanilla and beat until pale in
color, 2 to 3 minutes. In 3 increments, beat in the dry
ingredients alternately with the milk.

Pour into the prepared pans, smooth the tops, and
bake for about 35 minutes, or until the tops spring back
when lightly touched. A toothpick inserted in the center
of a cake should come out clean. Transfer the pans to
wire racks and let cool for 5 minutes. Run a knife
around the edges to loosen the cakes from the pans and
unmold onto the racks. Place one layer right side up. Let
cool completely.

Meanwhile, make the frosting: In a medium, heavy
saucepan, combine the sugar and cream. Place over
medium heat and, stirring constantly, bring to a boil.
Reduce heat to low and simmer for 10 minutes without
stirring. Remove from heat and stir in the chocolate,
butter, and vanilla, continuing to stir until the chocolate
and butter melt. Pour into a bowl and let cool to room
temperature, stirring occasionally. Refrigerate, stirring
frequently, until thickened to a good spreading consistency.

Place one layer, upside down, on a serving plate and
spread with 1¼ cups of the frosting. Place the second
layer on top, right side up, and frost the top and sides
with the remaining frosting. Refrigerate to set the frosting, but serve at room temperature.

Comforts Coconut Cake
with Cream Cheese and Coconut Frosting

🎂

THIS LOCALLY FAMOUS CAKE IS FROM GLENN MIWA'S COMFORTS, A TAKE-OUT SHOP
IN SAN ANSELMO, CALIFORNIA. IT IS ALWAYS KEPT ON HAND TO BUY
BY THE SLICE OR AS CUPCAKES, AND IT IS THEIR MOST-REQUESTED CAKE FOR SPECIAL
OCCASIONS. IF YOU MAKE YOUR OWN, GLENN POINTS OUT, THE
INTOXICATING FRAGRANCE OF COCONUT AND VANILLA WILL FILL YOUR KITCHEN WHEN THE
CAKE IS DONE, JUST AS IT DOES AT COMFORTS. THE COMFORTS COCONUT CAKE
IS A FAVORITE MARIN COUNTY CHOICE FOR BIRTHDAY CAKES; HERE IT IS DECORATED
TO STAR AT A LITTLE GIRL'S BIRTHDAY.

MAKES ONE
9-INCH 2-LAYER
CAKE; SERVES 12

3½ cups cake flour
1 tablespoon baking powder
¾ teaspoon salt
¾ cup (1½ sticks) unsalted butter at
   room temperature
1¾ cups granulated sugar
4 large eggs, separated, at room
   temperature
1 teaspoon vanilla extract
1 teaspoon coconut extract
One 14-ounce can coconut milk
¼ teaspoon cream of tartar

CREAM CHEESE AND COCONUT
FROSTING:
10½ ounces cream cheese at room
   temperature
½ cup (1 stick) unsalted butter at
   room temperature
1 teaspoon vanilla extract
5 cups confectioners' sugar, sifted
Pinch of salt
One 7-ounce package sweetened
   shredded coconut

MAKES 3 CUPS,
ENOUGH TO
FROST 1 CAKE

Preheat the oven to 350°F. Line the bottoms of two 9-by-2-inch cake pans with rounds of waxed paper.

Sift the flour, baking powder, and salt into a large bowl. In another large bowl, using an electric mixer on medium speed, beat the butter until smooth. Gradually beat in the sugar until light and fluffy. Beat in the egg yolks one at a time. Stir in the vanilla and coconut extracts.

With the mixer on low speed, add the dry ingredients to the butter mixture alternately with the coconut milk, beginning and ending with the dry ingredients. Beat just until combined.

Using clean beaters and a large bowl, beat the egg whites with the cream of tartar until medium-firm peaks form. Stir one-third of the whites into the batter to lighten it, then gently fold in the remaining whites.

Divide the batter evenly between the prepared pans and smooth the tops. Bake for about 30 minutes, or until a toothpick inserted into the center of each layer comes out clean. Transfer the pans to wire racks and let cool for 15 minutes. Run a small, sharp knife around the sides to loosen the cakes and unmold them onto the wire racks. Peel off the waxed paper. Let cool completely. (To make in advance, wrap the layers tightly in plastic wrap and store at room temperature for up to 24 hours.) CONTINUED

To make the frosting: In a large bowl, using an electric mixer, beat the cream cheese and butter together until smooth. Beat in the vanilla. Gradually beat in the confectioners' sugar and salt until well blended.

To frost, place 1 cake layer on a cake stand or plate. Tuck waxed paper strips under the cake to protect the stand or plate (see page 21). Spread about ¼ cup of the frosting over the top (enough to cover the cake) and sprinkle with ½ cup of the coconut. Top with the second cake layer. Spread the remaining frosting over the top and sides of the cake. Lightly press the remaining coconut over the top and sides of the cake to cover it completely. Remove the waxed paper strips. (To make in advance, wrap airtight in plastic wrap, then aluminum foil, and freeze for up to 1 week. Let stand at room temperature for 2 hours before serving.)

VARIATION: Use Lemon Curd (page 92) to fill the cake in place of the frosting.

DECORATING TIP: For a little girl's birthday, decorate the cake with tiny pink roses, plastic ballerinas, and long pink French birthday candles (as shown on page 83).

COMFORTS COCONUT CUPCAKES: Butter 24 standard muffin cups or line them with paper liners. Fill each cup three-fourths full with batter. Bake in a preheated 350°F oven for about 25 minutes, or until a toothpick inserted in the center of a cupcake comes out clean. Frost with the frosting and sprinkle with coconut. Makes 24 cupcakes.

Rum Toddy for a Cake

I like to split a cake baked in an oblong pan or in two round layers,
and fill it with a thick pastry cream flavored with lemon
or orange, and dust it at the last minute before serving. A little jam is
good on the inner slices before the cream goes on.
And a plain yellow cake in a spring mold, pricked when fresh
from the oven and bathed with the following booster,
is pleasing to all but the teetotalers.

—M. F. K. Fisher,
from *With Bold Knife and Fork*

½ cup packed brown sugar
1 cup fresh orange juice
⅓ cup dark rum

Dissolve sugar in orange juice over low heat.
Remove, add rum, and pour slowly over hot cake. Let stand
in tube pan or spring mold until cool.

Lindsey's Chocolate Cake

AN ALMOST-FLOURLESS CHOCOLATE CAKE, ALSO CALLED A FALLEN-SOUFFLÉ CAKE,
FROM LINDSEY SHERE, THE FOUNDING PASTRY CHEF AT ALICE WATERS'S CHEZ PANISSE
AND A COFOUNDER OF DOWNTOWN BAKERY IN HEALDSBURG, CALIFORNIA.
DARK AND SUMPTUOUS, THIS CAKE IS ONE OF THE FAVORITES AT THE
CHEZ PANISSE CAFÉ. LINDSEY STARTED HER PASTRY CAREER IN HIGH SCHOOL, WHEN SHE
BEGAN MAKING BIRTHDAY CAKES FOR HER BROTHERS AND SISTERS.
TODAY, SHE MAKES BIRTHDAY CAKES LIKE THIS ONE FOR HER FRIENDS AND FAMILY.
USE THE BEST-POSSIBLE CHOCOLATE TO MAKE THIS CAKE.

MAKES ONE
9-INCH CAKE;
SERVES 8 TO 10

1 cup (2 sticks) plus 2 tablespoons
salted butter
7½ ounces bittersweet chocolate,
chopped
1½ ounces unsweetened chocolate,
chopped
6 large eggs, separated, at room
temperature

1 cup plus 2 tablespoons granulated
sugar
6 tablespoons cake flour
½ teaspoon cream of tartar
Confectioners' sugar for dusting
Whipped cream (page 101) or ice cream
for serving

Preheat the oven to 350°F. Butter the sides and bottom of a 9-inch round cake pan. Line the bottom with a round of parchment paper or waxed paper. Butter the paper and dust the sides and bottom of the pan with flour, shaking out the excess.

In a double boiler over barely simmering water, melt the butter. Add the chocolate and stir occasionally until the chocolate is melted and the mixture is very smooth. Remove from heat and let cool slightly.

In a small bowl, beat the egg yolks just until blended. Beat in the granulated sugar until just mixed. Whisk the yolk mixture into the warm chocolate mixture. Fold in the flour until blended.

In a large bowl, beat the egg whites until frothy. Add the cream of tartar and continue beating until soft, rounded peaks form. Fold the egg whites quickly into the chocolate mixture, taking care not to deflate them.

Pour the batter into the prepared pan and bake for 45 to 50 minutes, or until the sides are set but the center of the cake is still soft. Remove from the oven and let cool completely in the pan on a wire rack. The cake will develop cracks in the top as it bakes, and more will appear as it cools, but this is normal. When the cake has cooled to

room temperature, you may cover the pan tightly with aluminum foil if you are not serving it right away. It will keep for a day or two.

To serve, unmold the cake, peel off the paper, and place the cake on a plate, the more presentable side up. Dust with confectioners' sugar and serve with whipped cream or ice cream.

NOTE: To make the crown, use the template on page 138, cutting the pattern from heavy kraft paper. Place the stencil over the cake and dust evenly with confectioners' sugar (see page 24), then remove the stencil.

Pavlova

THIS CLASSIC PAVLOVA FROM THE LATE RICHARD SAX'S *CLASSIC HOME DESSERTS*
IS A GOOD CHOICE FOR A NOT-TOO-SWEET, NONCONFORMIST BIRTHDAY "CAKE."
ANY ONE OF THE FRUIT COMBINATIONS SUGGESTED AT THE END OF THE RECIPE IS SURE TO
PLEASE YOUR GUESTS, OR YOU COULD USE THE LIST AS A GUIDE
FOR CREATING YOUR OWN COMBINATION OF WHATEVER FRUITS ARE IN SEASON.

This is Australia's contribution to the dessert world: a crunchy meringue shell filled with whipped cream and a rainbow of cut-up fresh fruits that will soften the meringue slightly. In England, Pavlova is served everywhere, frequently at dinner parties. The name honors the Russian ballerina Anna Pavlova, legendary for her role in Swan Lake. *Helen Mayer, a good cook who grew up in New Zealand and now lives in La Jolla, California, shared this recipe.*

—RICHARD SAX

MAKES ONE
8-INCH PAVLOVA;
SERVES 6

MERINGUE SHELL:
4 large egg whites (about ½ cup)
   at room temperature
Pinch of salt
½ cup sugar
1 teaspoon balsamic vinegar
½ teaspoon vanilla extract
1 tablespoon cornstarch

1 cup heavy cream, well chilled
Sliced or cut-up assorted fresh fruits
   (see list at end of recipe)

To make the meringue shell: Preheat the oven to 400°F. Using a plate or an 8-inch cake pan as a guide, trace an 8-inch circle onto a sheet of parchment paper or waxed paper. Invert the paper onto a baking sheet and butter the paper lightly; set aside.

Using an electric mixer or a whisk, beat the egg whites with the salt in a medium bowl on medium-high speed until foamy. Gradually beat in the sugar; beat in the vinegar and vanilla. Continue beating until the meringue forms stiff, glossy peaks. Sift the cornstarch over the meringue and fold it in gently.

Heap the meringue onto the parchment paper, swirling it out with the back of a spoon to fill the 8-inch circle, forming high sides around the edge and leaving a wide indentation in the center.

Place the baking sheet with the meringue in the oven and immediately lower the temperature to 225°F. Bake, undisturbed, for 1½ to 2 hours, or until set but still somewhat soft when pressed lightly with a fingertip. Transfer the shell to a wire rack and let cool completely, about 30 minutes. (You can bake the meringue early in the day and leave it, loosely covered, at room temperature.)

Shortly before serving, whip the cream in a chilled bowl until nearly stiff. Top the meringue with the whipped cream; arrange the fruit attractively over the top.

Good Fruit Combinations for Pavlova

• Nectarines, blueberries, kiwis, raspberries
• Peaches, plums, golden raspberries, blackberries
• Mangoes, bananas, oranges, pink grapefruit
• Red currants, blackberries, plums, strawberries
• Apples, pears, grapes, dried cranberries
• Pineapple, passion fruit, grated coconut

OUR NOTE: You could also try other fillings, such as Lemon Curd (page 92), ice cream, or Cocoa Whipped Cream Frosting (page 39; try this with raspberries).

OUR VARIATION: Mix the fruit together 10 minutes before serving. Stir in 1 tablespoon sugar and 1 to 2 teaspoons fresh lemon juice (to taste). Let stand for 10 minutes. Add ½ teaspoon vanilla extract and 1 to 2 tablespoons sugar (to taste) to the whipped cream; fold in until blended. Fill the meringue with the cream and top with the fruit, as in the master recipe.

Cream Puffs with Lemon Filling

CREAM PUFFS MAKE AN UNUSUAL BUT INNOVATIVE BIRTHDAY "CAKE" THAT WILL APPEAL TO
CHILDREN (BECAUSE THEY CAN EAT THEM OUT OF HAND) AND AT THE
SAME TIME IS A SOPHISTICATED ALTERNATIVE FOR ADULTS. THESE PUFFS, CONTRIBUTED
BY PASTRY CHEFS KATHLEEN STEWART AND DAVID LEBOVITZ TO
THE BAKER'S DOZEN COOKBOOK, ARE SERVED ON A POOL OF CARAMEL SAUCE. TO SERVE
AT A BIRTHDAY CELEBRATION, STACK THE PUFFS IN A PYRAMID
ON A CAKE PLATE, WITH CANDLES INSERTED IN THE TOPS OF THE EXPOSED PUFFS
(OR SEE DAVID'S SUGGESTION, BELOW).

*I have fond memories of cream puffs. When my Danish grandmother came to visit my family
when I was a child, she transformed our suburban kitchen into a cream puff bakery. She spooned the sticky batter
onto baking sheets, and they gloriously rose and puffed in the oven. Once cool, they were filled
with whipped cream. When she left, our freezer would be packed with carefully sealed packs of cream puffs;
often I would eat them right out of the freezer.*

*Today, I like to serve cream puffs for birthdays, as they are so adaptable. I like to serve
mounds of them coated with chocolate sauce and sprinkled with toasted sliced almonds. Each birthday guest gets his
or her own creation with a candle to make birthday wishes come true.*

—DAVID LEBOVITZ

MAKES ABOUT
2 DOZEN PUFFS;
SERVES 6 TO 8

CREAM PUFFS:
1 cup water
6 tablespoons unsalted butter, cut into
    small pieces
1 teaspoon sugar
¼ teaspoon salt
1 cup all-purpose flour
4 large eggs at room temperature
1 large egg yolk beaten with 2 teaspoons
    milk, for the glaze

LEMON FILLING:
1 cup heavy cream
1 cup Lemon Curd (recipe follows)

1 cup Caramel Sauce (recipe follows)

Preheat the oven to 425°F. Place an oven rack in the center of the oven. Line a baking sheet with parchment paper or use an ungreased baking sheet.

In a medium saucepan, combine the water, butter, sugar, and salt. Bring to a boil over medium heat, stirring often to be sure the butter is completely melted by the time the water boils. Add the flour all at once, beating well, and continue stirring until the paste forms a mass that comes away from the sides of the pan, about 30 seconds. Remove from heat.

Transfer the paste to the bowl of a heavy-duty mixer fitted with the paddle attachment, or to a medium bowl. Let stand for 3 minutes to cool the paste slightly. On low speed, one at a time, beat in the eggs, making sure each egg is incorporated before adding the next. The dough will be stiff and shiny.

Transfer the dough to a pastry bag fitted with a ½-inch-wide plain tip. Pipe the dough into 2-inch-diameter mounds about 1½ inches high and about 2 inches apart on the prepared pan. Lightly the brush the tips of the

CONTINUED

mounds with the egg mixture, tamping down the pointed tips as you go. Be careful not to let the glaze drip down onto the pan, or it will harden during baking and prevent the puffs from reaching their full expansion.

Put the puffs in the oven and immediately lower the oven temperature to 375°F. Bake for 25 to 30 minutes, or until golden brown. Remove from the oven and turn the oven off.

Using the tip of a small, sharp knife, pierce the side of each puff to release steam. Return the puffs to the oven for 5 minutes. Remove from the oven and let cool completely on the pan before filling. (The puffs can be baked up to 1 day ahead and stored in an airtight container at room temperature, or frozen for up to 3 months. To reheat and crisp the puffs, bake on a baking sheet in a preheated 350°F oven until heated through, about 5 minutes for room-temperature puffs and 10 minutes for frozen puffs. No need to thaw frozen puffs before reheating.)

To make the filling: In a chilled deep bowl, beat the cream until very stiff peaks form. Fold in the lemon curd until blended. Transfer to a pastry bag fitted with a bismarck tip (see note) or a ½-inch-wide plain tip.

If using a bismarck tip, pierce the bottom of each puff and pipe in the filling. If using a plain tip, split each puff almost, but not fully, in half through its equator. Pipe the filling into the bottom of each puff, then replace the top. (The filled puffs can be prepared up to 2 hours ahead, loosely covered with plastic wrap, and refrigerated.)

To serve, spoon equal amounts of the caramel sauce on 6 to 8 dessert plates. Arrange 3 or 4 puffs in the center of the sauce and serve immediately.

NOTE: A bismarck tip, available at bakery supply shops, is a pastry tip shaped like a long nozzle. It is perfect for squirting cream or jelly into puffs or doughnuts.

LEMON CURD
Makes about 1½ cups

2 large eggs at room temperature
3 large egg yolks at room temperature
Grated zest of 4 lemons
¾ cup fresh lemon juice (about 4 lemons)
6 tablespoons cold unsalted butter, cut into ½-inch cubes
¾ cup sugar
2 tablespoons water

In a medium, heavy saucepan, combine all the ingredients. Using a heat-resistant silicone or wooden spatula, stir constantly over medium-low heat, being careful not to let the mixture come to a boil, until it is thick enough to coat the spatula and a trail is left when you run a finger through it, about 7 minutes (an instant-read thermometer inserted in the mixture will read 185°F). Do not overcook; the curd will thicken as it cools. Immediately strain the curd through a fine-mesh sieve into a bowl.

Press a sheet of plastic wrap directly onto the surface of the curd. With the tip of a sharp knife, poke a few holes in the plastic to allow steam to escape. Let cool to room temperature. Transfer to an airtight container and refrigerate for up to 5 days.

CARAMEL SAUCE
Makes 1¾ cups

½ cup cold water
1 cup sugar
¼ teaspoon fresh lemon juice
¼ cup boiling water
½ cup heavy cream at room temperature
4 tablespoons unsalted butter at room temperature
1 tablespoon corn syrup

Pour the cold water into a medium, heavy saucepan. Add the sugar and lemon juice and stir just enough to dampen the sugar. Cover and bring to a boil over medium heat, swirling the pan by the handle to help dissolve the sugar. Occasionally press a wet pastry brush against any sugar crystals that form on the sides of the pan to wash them back into the syrup.

Uncover the pan and increase the heat to medium-high. Cook until the caramel is a deep red brown (about the color of an old penny). Standing back to avoid splashes and steam, immediately pour the boiling water into the caramel. If the caramel hardens, whisk over low heat to dissolve.

Remove from heat and whisk in the cream; the mixture will bubble up, so be careful. Return to low heat and whisk until the hardened caramel dissolves. Add the butter and corn syrup and whisk until the sauce comes to a boil. Strain to remove any undissolved sugar crystals. Whisk again before serving. Serve warm, at room temperature, or chilled.

OUR VARIATIONS: For a simpler version of this "cake" that will particularly appeal to children, replace the lemon filling with 2 cups Pastry Cream (page 71), Whipped Cream Frosting (page 95), or Cocoa Whipped Cream Frosting (page 39), or fill the puffs at the last minute with your choice of ice cream. Serve with a chocolate sauce made by warming the Fast Fudge Frosting from Alice Medrich's Fastest Fudge Cake (page 54).

The Elvis Cake

♛

BAKER MARIA BRUSCINO SANCHEZ'S RECIPE, FROM HER BOOK
SWEET MARIA'S CAKE KITCHEN, WAS INSPIRED BY THE KING'S FAVORITE SANDWICH.
SHE TRIES TO MAKE THIS CAKE EVERY YEAR ON JANUARY 8, ELVIS'S BIRTHDAY.

MAKES ONE
9-INCH 2-LAYER
CAKE; SERVES
8 TO 10

DEVIL'S FOOD LAYER CAKE:
1 cup boiling water
1 cup unsweetened cocoa powder
2 cups all-purpose flour
1¾ cups sugar
1½ teaspoons baking soda
2 teaspoons baking powder
1 teaspoon salt
2 eggs

1 cup buttermilk
½ cup vegetable oil
2 teaspoons vanilla extract

Whipped Cream Frosting (recipe follows)
1 cup smooth peanut butter, plus more
   for garnish
1 large banana, plus more for garnish
Unsweetened cocoa powder for dusting

To make the cake: Preheat the oven to 350°F. Grease and flour two 9-inch round cake pans, knocking out the excess flour, or line them with parchment paper.

In a small bowl, pour the boiling water over the cocoa. Set aside to cool.

In an electric mixer, combine the flour, sugar, baking soda, baking powder, and salt. Mix on low speed. Add the eggs and cocoa mixture and blend on low speed for 1 minute. Scrape down the sides and bottom of the bowl. Add the buttermilk, oil, and vanilla. Beat on low speed for 1 minute. Scrape down the bowl. Beat on medium speed for 1 to 2 minutes, or until smooth.

Pour the batter evenly into the prepared pans. Bake for 20 to 25 minutes, or until a tester comes out with a fine crumb. Remove the pans from the oven and place on wire racks. Let the cakes cool in the pans for 5 to 10 minutes. Carefully remove the cakes from the pans and place on wire racks. Let cool completely before frosting. Remove and discard the parchment paper before decorating.

Level off the tops of the 2 chocolate layers. Place one layer, cut side up, on a serving plate. Spread a thin layer of whipped cream over the layer. Drop spoonfuls of the peanut butter on top of the thin cream layer. Slice the banana and arrange in the center of the cake. Place the other layer, cut side down, on top of the peanut butter and bananas. Press gently.

Using a metal icing spatula, frost the cake with the remaining whipped cream frosting, using swirling strokes. Start at the top and continue to spread down the sides of the cake. Refrigerate the cake. Before serving, garnish each slice with 1 teaspoon of peanut butter and a few slices of banana, and dust with unsweetened cocoa powder. Serve chilled.

WHIPPED CREAM FROSTING
Makes 4 cups, enough to fill and frost one 9-inch 2-layer round cake

2 cups heavy cream
¼ cup sugar

In an electric mixer with a wire whisk attachment, beat the cream for 2 to 3 minutes, until soft peaks form. Add the sugar and beat until stiff peaks form.

Magic Spice Cake
with Penuche Frosting

ELOISE KLEINMAN ADAPTED THIS SHEET-CAKE RECIPE FROM ONE BY MRS. K. J. BARNELL
IN *COOKING CAN BE FUN*, PUBLISHED BY THE MESSIAH LUTHERAN CHURCH IN 1949.
IT'S DELICIOUSLY SPICY AND TOPPED WITH A BROWN SUGAR FROSTING.

*My mom's baking career began at a young age. When she was twelve, she won first place for the white cake she
entered in her town fair. During my childhood years, with a swarm of kids always about,
she continued to bake for family and friends. Of course, in our home everyone had a favorite birthday cake.
Dad's favorite was this spice cake with penuche frosting. Mom baked it in her covered
rectangular cake pan, which was easy to hide from any little ones who might have tried to sneak a finger in
the icing for a quick taste before the cake was served.* —KATHRYN KLEINMAN

1 cup granulated sugar
¾ cup packed light brown sugar
¾ cup (1½ sticks) unsalted butter at
    room temperature
1 cup buttermilk
2¼ cups cake flour
1 teaspoon salt
1 teaspoon baking powder
¾ teaspoon baking soda
½ teaspoon ground cloves
½ teaspoon ground nutmeg
¾ teaspoon ground cinnamon
3 large eggs, beaten

PENUCHE FROSTING:
1 cup packed light brown sugar
½ cup granulated sugar
⅓ cup milk
4 tablespoons unsalted butter
1 tablespoon white corn syrup
¼ teaspoon salt
1 teaspoon vanilla extract

Preheat the oven to 350°F. Butter and flour two 9-inch round cake pans or one 9-by-13-inch pan; knock out the excess flour.

In a large bowl, combine the sugars and butter. Beat until light and fluffy. Stir in the buttermilk and beat until smooth. Sift the flour, salt, baking powder, baking soda, and spices together onto a sheet of waxed paper. Gradually beat the dry ingredients into the wet ingredients and beat until smooth. Add the eggs and beat again until smooth.

Pour the batter into the prepared pan(s) and smooth the top(s) with a rubber spatula. Bake the 9-inch layers for 30 to 35 minutes or the 9-by-13-inch cake for 45 minutes, or until a cake tester or toothpick inserted in the center comes out clean. Let the layers cool in the pans for 10 minutes, then unmold onto wire racks and let cool completely; let the 9-by-13-inch cake cool completely in the pan.

To make the frosting: Combine all the ingredients except the vanilla in a medium saucepan. Bring to a boil over medium heat and boil briskly for 1 minute while stirring. Remove from heat and let cool to lukewarm. Stir in the vanilla and beat with a wooden spoon until thick enough to spread.

Fill and frost the layers or frost the sheet cake in the pan.

True Sponge Cake

❋

UNLIKE SOME RECIPES, WHICH ADD BAKING POWDER FOR INSURANCE,
THIS IS A "TRUE" SPONGE CAKE THAT IS LEAVENED ONLY BY WELL-BEATEN EGGS.
HERE IT IS FROSTED WITH BUTTERCREAM FROSTING.

*I was happy when Kathryn Kleinman asked me to write the text for this book, because I love
to make birthday cakes; I have had some friends burst into tears because they were so touched when their cake
appeared. I always use this easy sponge cake recipe from Marion Cunningham's
Fannie Farmer's Cookbook, filling it with raspberry jam, frosting it with buttercream frosting, and decorating
it with fresh flowers and silver dragées.*
—CAROLYN MILLER

MAKES ONE
9-INCH TUBE CAKE
OR ONE 8-INCH
2-LAYER CAKE;
SERVES 10 TO 12

5 large eggs, separated
1 tablespoon fresh lemon juice
1 cup sugar
¼ teaspoon salt
1 cup cake flour

Preheat the oven to 325°F. Line the bottom of a 9-inch tube pan or two 8-inch round cake pans with a round of waxed paper.

In a medium bowl, beat the egg yolks with the lemon juice until pale and thick. Gradually beat in ¾ cup of the sugar.

In a large bowl, beat the egg whites until foamy. Add the salt and beat until the whites form soft peaks. Gradually beat in the remaining ¼ cup sugar and continue beating until the whites form stiff, glossy peaks.

Stir one-fourth of the whites into the yolk mixture. Spoon the remaining whites over the yolk mixture and sift the flour on top. Gently fold until blended.

Spoon the batter into the prepared pan(s) and smooth the top. Bake for 45 to 55 minutes in the tube pan, 25 to 30 minutes in the layer pans, or until a toothpick inserted in the center comes out clean. Invert the pan(s) onto a wire rack and let the cake cool completely before unmolding.

Dust with confectioners' sugar, sifted through a sieve, or frost with lemon-flavored confectioners' frosting or any other light frosting you wish.

BUTTERCREAM FROSTING (from Carolyn Miller):
Makes about 2 cups, enough to frost an 8-inch 2-layer cake

1 large organic egg yolk (optional; see note)
1⅓ cups sifted confectioners' sugar
2 teaspoons vanilla extract
¾ cup (1½ sticks) unsalted butter at room temperature

In a warmed large bowl, combine all the ingredients. Beat at medium speed until smooth, about 5 minutes. Refrigerate until thick enough to use.

DECORATING TIP: Reserve ½ cup of the frosting; tint a pale lavender with a tiny bit of red and blue food coloring. Fill the cake with raspberry jam.

Frost the cake with the remaining frosting. Use a star pastry tip to make a fluted border of lavender frosting on the top and bottom edges of the cake, and a small plain tip to write birthday greetings on the top. Decorate the cake with fresh purple violas or violets and tiny silver dragées, and top with long white French birthday candles. Dust the edges of the cake plate with confectioners' sugar and sprinkle with more flowers.

NOTE: If you are concerned about eating or serving food containing raw egg, don't use the egg yolk.

Beth's Very Berry Shortcake

BETH SETRAKIAN FOUNDED BETH'S FINE DESSERTS IN MILL VALLEY, CALIFORNIA, IN 1988, WHEN HER CHILDREN WERE JUST BABIES. IN FACT, THE ORIGINAL PACKAGING FOR BETH'S BABIES HEAVENLY LITTLE COOKIES FEATURED HER CHILDREN, NICHOLAS AND SOPHIA, DEPICTED AS CHERUBS. TODAY, BETH'S COOKIES AND CAKE MIXES ARE SOLD THROUGHOUT THE COUNTRY IN SPECIALTY FOODS STORES.

I grew up with three brothers and two sisters, and we each had a favorite birthday cake, which my mother lovingly prepared. She was an excellent baker and always preferred using seasonal ingredients. My own birthday is in January, which calls for something rich and chocolatey, but my favorite birthday cake is the shortcake she always made for my oldest brother, whose birthday is in July. She used to give us all a pail and send us out to collect wild blackberries at the peak of their season. The collected berries would be transformed into a wild-blackberry birthday shortcake. The delicious crumble of the shortcake, the tanginess of the berries, and the creamy dollops of whipped cream were a midsummer dream!

—BETH SETRAKIAN

MAKES ONE 9-INCH 2-LAYER CAKE; SERVES 10 TO 12

SHORTCAKE:
2 cups unbleached all-purpose flour
4 teaspoons baking powder
½ teaspoon salt
½ cup sugar
¾ cup (1½ sticks) cold unsalted butter, cut into ¼-inch dice
1 cup heavy cream or milk

BERRY FILLING AND TOPPING:
6 cups fresh seasonal berries, such as sliced hulled strawberries, blueberries, blackberries, raspberries, or a mixture
1 cup strawberry or seedless raspberry preserves, heated slightly until smooth, or fresh lemon juice and sugar to taste

FLAVORED WHIPPED CREAM:
2 cups heavy cream
3 tablespoons sugar
1 teaspoon vanilla extract

To make the shortcake: Preheat the oven to 400°F. Line the bottom of a 9-inch round cake pan with parchment paper.

In a medium bowl, combine the flour, baking powder, salt, and sugar. Stir to blend. Using an electric mixer fitted with the paddle attachment, or a pastry cutter or 2 dinner knives, cut the butter into the flour mixture until it resembles coarse meal. Add the cream or milk all at once and stir to blend. Knead gently in the bowl for less than a minute to form a soft dough. Very lightly press the dough into the prepared pan. Bake for about 20 minutes, or until golden brown. Let cool slightly, then unmold onto a rack to cool completely.

To make the berry filling and topping: Reserve half of the berries for the topping. For the filling, put the remaining berries in a large bowl and add the warm preserves or the lemon juice and sugar. Stir to blend and set aside.

Using a long serrated knife, carefully cut the shortcake horizontally into 2 equal layers. Place the bottom layer on a serving plate or stand. Top with the berry filling. Place the second layer on top of the berries.

In a deep bowl, combine all the ingredients for the flavored whipped cream and beat until soft peaks form. Spoon the whipped cream over the shortcake. Top with the reserved berries, allowing them to cascade over the sides of the cake. Serve at once.

Pineapple Upside-Down Cake

RESTAURATEUR AND COOKBOOK AUTHOR CINDY PAWLCYN WAS THRILLED
WHEN THE STAFF AT WILLIAMS-SONOMA CALLED, ASKING HER TO MAKE PINEAPPLE
UPSIDE-DOWN CAKES FOR COMPANY FOUNDER CHUCK WILLIAMS'S
EIGHTIETH BIRTHDAY. THIS CAKE, AN OLD AMERICAN FAVORITE, IS A GOOD BIRTHDAY
TREAT FOR ANYONE, LIKE CHUCK, WHO LOVES GOOD HOME COOKING.

*For my eightieth birthday, seven years ago, a dinner was held in the Bay Café area of
Williams-Sonoma for some of my old friends and coworkers. I was only told there was to be a dinner, but no details
were revealed. So I was completely surprised when dessert was served. My birthday cake was
pineapple upside-down cake baked by Cindy Pawlcyn at the Fog City Diner, one of my favorite restaurants.
Pineapple upside-down cake being my all-time favorite cake from my childhood, I was pleased
to find it at the Fog City Diner soon after it opened many years ago. It was one of their special desserts and not
always on the menu. Some of my coworkers knew of my affection for the cake, so they called Cindy
and asked if the restaurant could supply the cakes. The result was that Cindy baked fifteen
or more pineapple upside-down cakes on my birthday and delivered them warm for my birthday dinner.
Yes, they were delicious and certainly a very special part of my birthday.* —CHUCK WILLIAMS

MAKES ONE
12-INCH CAKE;
SERVES 12
GENEROUSLY

TOPPING:
1 small ripe pineapple (3½ to 4
   pounds)
6 tablespoons unsalted butter
1 cup firmly packed dark brown sugar
1 cup pitted fresh or brandied cherries,
   halved, or pecan halves

BATTER:
3¾ cups sifted cake flour
2 teaspoons baking powder
1½ teaspoons salt
¾ cup (1½ sticks) unsalted butter at
   room temperature
2½ cups granulated sugar
3 large eggs
1 tablespoon vanilla extract
1½ cups milk
⅓ cup dark rum

Sweetened whipped cream (page 95)
   or ice cream for serving

Place an oven rack in the upper third of the oven. Preheat
the oven to 350°F.

To make the topping: Slice off the top and bottom of
the pineapple so you have a stable base. Place the pineapple on end and use a large knife to cut down the side,
removing the skin. Use a paring knife to cut out the
"eyes." Cut the pineapple lengthwise into 4 wedges and
cut out the core. Cut the wedges into ⅜-inch-thick slices
and set aside.

In a 12-inch cast-iron skillet, melt the butter over medium heat, then sprinkle in the brown sugar. Cook just until the mixture begins to bubble, then remove from heat. The mixture will continue to cook, so take care not to overcook it. Arrange the pineapple slices in tightly spaced concentric circles in the pan. Tuck the cherries or pecans into the spaces between the pineapple slices. Set aside.

To make the batter: Sift the flour, baking powder, and salt together onto a sheet of waxed paper. In a large bowl, using a wooden spoon, or in a heavy-duty mixer fitted with a paddle attachment, cream the butter and sugar together until light and fluffy. Beat in the eggs one at a time. Beat in the vanilla. Combine the milk and rum in a large measuring cup. Add the dry ingredients and milk mixture alternately in small increments, starting and ending with the dry ingredients. Stir or mix on low speed until blended. If using a mixer, remove the paddle and scrape down the paddle and sides of the bowl with a rubber spatula and stir to blend the batter evenly.

Pour the batter over the fruit in the pan. Smooth the top with a rubber spatula. The pan will be quite full and some of the liquid may peek out at the edges. Place the pan on the upper rack, and place a baking sheet lined with parchment paper on a lower rack to catch any drips. Bake for 50 to 60 minutes, or until the cake is springy to the touch and a toothpick inserted in the center comes out clean. Let cool in the pan for about 3 minutes, then invert onto a large cake plate. Use a spatula to remove any caramel or fruit in the pan.

Serve warm, with sweetened whipped cream or ice cream.

VARIATIONS: Replace the pineapple with 5 or 6 large plums or apricots, pitted and quartered, or 3 to 4 large peaches or pears, pitted or cored and quartered. Replace the cherries or pecans with whole blanched almonds.

Lincoln Log Cake

SHERRY FALKNER AND
ELIZABETH FALKNER

ELIZABETH FALKNER CREATED A STIR AMONG BAY AREA FOOD-LOVERS WHEN SHE OPENED
CITIZEN CAKE, HER PASTRY SHOP AND RESTAURANT, IN SAN FRANCISCO IN
1997. SINCE THEN, CITIZEN CAKE HAS BECOME ONE OF THE CITY'S FAVORITE SOURCES FOR
ALL KINDS OF PASTRIES, INCLUDING UNUSUAL BIRTHDAY CAKES.
ELIZABETH'S CONTEMPORARY TAKE ON PASTRIES INCLUDES IMAGINATIVE MODERNIST
CAKES THAT REFLECT HER TRAINING AS A FINE ARTS STUDENT, AND
THE EVEN EARLIER INFLUENCE OF HER MOTHER SHERRY'S LINCOLN LOG CAKE.

*My birthday is February 12 (also Abraham Lincoln's birthday), so I always asked my mom for
this homemade ice cream cake with chocolate ganache and coffee ice cream. These were two of my favorite flavors
growing up, and they still are. For my thirty-seventh birthday, my friends and mom surprised me with a
great party, and my mom made me the Lincoln Log cake, which I have described to all of my friends over the years.*

—ELIZABETH FALKNER

MAKES ONE
15-INCH-LONG
CAKE ROLL;
SERVES 10

4 large eggs, separated
½ teaspoon kosher salt
½ teaspoon cream of tartar
⅓ cup plus ¾ cup granulated sugar
¼ cup water
1 teaspoon vanilla extract
½ cup unsweetened cocoa powder
½ cup Wondra instant flour or sifted
  cake flour
¼ teaspoon baking soda
Sifted confectioners' sugar for
  sprinkling

FILLING:
1 quart of your favorite ice cream (see
  note) or 1 cup heavy cream whipped
  with 1 cup marshmallow cream

CHOCOLATE GANACHE:
1 cup heavy cream
¾ cup semisweet or bittersweet
  chocolate pieces

Preheat the oven to 350°F. Brush a 10-by-15-inch jelly roll pan with melted butter or spray with vegetable-oil cooking spray. Line with parchment paper.

In a large bowl, beat the egg whites with the salt and cream of tartar until soft peaks form. Gradually beat in the ⅓ cup sugar and continue beating until stiff, glossy peaks form.

In a medium bowl, combine the egg yolks, the ¾ cup sugar, the water, and vanilla. Beat until smooth. Sift the cocoa, flour, and baking soda together onto a sheet of waxed paper. Add the dry ingredients to the wet ingredients and beat until blended, about 1 minute. Using a rubber spatula, gently fold the beaten egg whites into the batter until blended.

Pour into the prepared pan, smooth the top, and bake on the center rack of the oven for 20 to 25 minutes, or until the cake springs back when touched lightly in the center with your finger.

Lay out a kitchen towel or a piece of parchment paper and sprinkle it with confectioners' sugar. Unmold the hot cake onto the towel or paper by turning the pan over and carefully pulling down on the paper lining. Trim the edges and roll up in the towel or paper. Let cool completely.

CONTINUED

To fill the cake, if using ice cream, let the ice cream stand at room temperature for about 20 minutes to soften slightly to spreading consistency. Remove the towel or paper from the cake. Unroll the cake on a work surface with one of the long sides nearest you and spread the cake evenly with the filling, leaving the last inch on the far end uncovered. Roll the cake up into a jelly roll shape, beginning with the long side nearest you, and cover it in plastic wrap. Place in the freezer, seam side down, until frozen, about 1 hour.

To make the ganache: In a small saucepan, bring the cream to a boil. Pour over the chocolate in a bowl. Let stand until the chocolate has melted. Blend with a whisk until smooth.

Remove the cake from the freezer. Using an icing spatula, spread the ganache evenly over all the exposed surfaces. Let the ganache set until firm. Cover the cake with plastic wrap and return to the freezer. Freeze for at least 2 hours or for up to 2 weeks, until ready to present and serve (with candles).

OUR NOTE: Elizabeth recommends homemade Mocha Almond Fudge, Mocha Chip ice cream, or Häagen-Dazs.

♫♪

THE BIRTHDAY SONG

"THE BIRTHDAY SONG," OR "HAPPY BIRTHDAY TO YOU," WAS
ORIGINALLY PART OF A SONG CALLED "GOOD MORNING TO ALL,"
WRITTEN BY TWO SISTERS WHO WERE BOTH ELEMENTARY
SCHOOLTEACHERS. PATTY SMITH HILL WROTE THE LYRICS, AND
MILDRED J. HILL WROTE THE MUSIC; THE SONG WAS FIRST
PUBLISHED IN 1893. THOUGH THEIR NAMES ARE ONLY A FOOTNOTE
IN HISTORY, "HAPPY BIRTHDAY TO YOU" HAS BECOME ONE
OF THE WORLD'S BEST-KNOWN SONGS, AND NOW NO BIRTHDAY IS
COMPLETE WITHOUT IT BEING SUNG WHILE THE LIGHTED
BIRTHDAY CAKE IS PRESENTED TO THE CELEBRANT.

STEPHANIE GREENLEIGH
AND KATHRYN KLEINMAN

Pink Elephant Cutout Cake

The inspiration for this cake came from Carrie Brown, who owns the Jimtown Store near Healdsburg, California. She offered her prized elephant mold, which was used as a template for making the cake. Food stylist Stephanie Greenleigh decorated the little elephant with pink frosting and licorice candies. To continue the pink party theme, serve this cake with pink beverages: Shirley Temples and pink lemonade for children, and pink Champagne, kir, and/or cranberry Cosmopolitans for adults.

MAKES 1 LARGE
ELEPHANT-
SHAPED CAKE;
SERVES 20 TO 24

2 boxes white-cake mix
Ingredients called for in cake-mix
    instructions
Elephant template (page 139)
2 recipes Fluffy Frosting (page 122)
Licorice strings and pieces for decoration

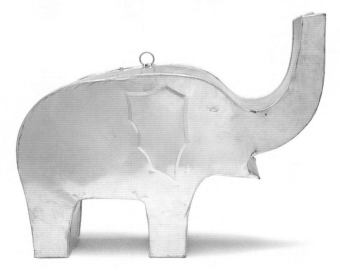

Preheat the oven according to the cake-mix instructions. Line the bottom of a 12-by-15-inch baking pan with parchment paper.

Combine the 2 cake mixes in a large bowl and prepare the batter according to the mix instructions.

Pour the batter into the prepared pan and bake for 45 to 55 minutes, or until a toothpick inserted in the center comes out clean. Remove from the oven and transfer the pan to a wire rack. Let cool completely.

Place a cardboard template in the shape of an elephant on top of the cake and cut around it with a small sharp knife. Remove the side pieces of cake and carefully unmold the elephant shape onto a large tray. Place strips of waxed paper under the edges of the cake to cover the tray. Frost the cake with the frosting, making peaks and swirls. Decorate with licorice string to form the ear and mouth, and use licorice pieces for the eye and toes. Remove the paper to serve.

Easiest Hot Fudge Pudding Cake

ALTHOUGH IT IS HOMEY-LOOKING RATHER THAN BEAUTIFUL, A CHOCOLATE PUDDING CAKE
IS A GLORIOUSLY FUDGY, QUICK, AND EASY-TO-MAKE CHOICE FOR A
BIRTHDAY CAKE: WHEN BAKED, THE BATTER SEPARATES INTO A THICK CHOCOLATE SAUCE
ON THE BOTTOM AND A BROWNIELIKE CAKE ON THE TOP.
SERVE IT WARM, IF POSSIBLE, ACCOMPANIED WITH VANILLA OR COFFEE ICE CREAM.
HERE, TERESA RETZLAFF, WHO DID MUCH OF THE RESEARCH FOR THIS BOOK,
TELLS HOW CHANCING ON AN ARTICLE ABOUT THIS CAKE IN
COOK'S ILLUSTRATED MAGAZINE BROUGHT BACK MEMORIES OF HER CHILDHOOD BIRTHDAY
CAKES, AND PRECIOUS RECOLLECTIONS OF HER MOTHER.

Last summer, my mother passed away. This year has been a strange and sentimental one for me. In early May, I started to think about my birthday coming up at the end of the month. It would be the first birthday that I would celebrate without Mom calling to wish me a wonderful day and share memories of that early morning back in 1966 when I arrived all in a hurry.

My mother was never a great cook, although she had a repertoire of meals that she did well. But back in the late 1960s, with four small children on her hands (I was the youngest), she relied heavily on boxed mixes to make things easier. I think she started making this cake because my brother didn't like frosting—it was just too sweet for him. All four of us loved this cake, though, and it was the birthday cake of choice in our house, served humbly in the pan in which it was baked, with little multicolored sprinkles on top to make it festive. I know Mom used a mix for it, because years later I asked her about it, and she told me the mix was no longer being made. I thought that was the end of it.

This May, I was hanging out in a bookstore, flipping through cooking magazines, thinking about Mom, and my birthday, and wondering what I felt like doing. I had a yearning for a good old-fashioned birthday party, like those magic ones we had when we were kids. I picked up a copy of Cook's Illustrated, *and lo and behold! there was a wonderful article about how to make the Easiest*

Hot Fudge Pudding Cake, with what looked like a very simple recipe. It felt like Mom was still looking out for me.

It was a marvelous party, with bubbles blown, and a great water-gun fight, and good friends, and a lot of laughter. And the best part was the cake: warm, gooey, and delicious, served in the pan with little colored sprinkles on it. Just like my mom used to make.

—TERESA RETZLAFF

Makes one 8-inch round or square cake; serves 8

Topping:
2 teaspoons instant coffee powder
1½ cups water
⅓ cup Dutch-processed cocoa powder
⅓ cup packed brown sugar
⅓ cup granulated sugar

6 tablespoons unsalted butter
⅓ cup Dutch-processed cocoa powder
2 ounces semisweet or bittersweet chocolate, chopped
¾ cup unbleached all-purpose flour
2 teaspoons baking powder
⅔ cup granulated sugar
1 tablespoon vanilla extract
⅓ cup whole milk
¼ teaspoon salt
1 large egg yolk

Adjust an oven rack in the lower third of the oven. Preheat the oven to 325°F. Lightly spray an 8-inch round or square glass baking dish with vegetable-oil cooking spray.

To make the topping: Stir the instant coffee into the water; set aside to dissolve. In a small bowl, combine the cocoa and sugars, breaking up the clumps of brown sugar with your fingers. Stir to blend. Set aside.

In a small metal bowl set over a saucepan of barely simmering water, combine the butter, cocoa, and chocolate. Heat until melted, then whisk until smooth. Remove from heat and set aside to cool slightly.

In a small bowl, combine the flour and baking powder. Whisk to blend. In a medium bowl, combine the sugar, vanilla, milk, and salt. Whisk until blended, then whisk in the egg yolk. Add the chocolate mixture and whisk to blend. Add the flour mixture and whisk until incorporated.

Pour the batter into the prepared baking dish and spread it evenly to the sides and corners. Sprinkle the cocoa topping mixture evenly over the batter to cover the entire surface. Pour the coffee mixture gently over the cocoa mixture. Bake until puffed, bubbling, and just beginning to pull away from the sides of the dish, about 45 minutes. Do not overbake. Transfer the dish to a wire rack and let the cake cool for about 25 minutes before serving.

Baby Cakes

BAKING EXPERT FLO BRAKER IS KNOWN FOR HER BOOKS *THE SIMPLE ART OF PERFECT BAKING* AND *SWEET MINIATURES*, AS WELL AS FOR HER "BABY CAKES," DELIGHTFUL 6-INCH TREATS JUST RIGHT FOR A BABY'S FIRST BIRTHDAY OR AS A SPECIAL GIFT FOR ONE PERSON. BABY CAKES COME IN TWO VERSIONS: ONE 2-LAYER AMERICAN-STYLE CAKE WITH BUTTERCREAM FILLING AND FROSTING, OR TWO SINGLE-LAYER EUROPEAN-STYLE CAKES COVERED WITH A GLAZE.

MAKES ONE 6-INCH 2-LAYER CAKE OR TWO 6-INCH SINGLE-LAYER CAKES; SERVES 4

1 cup cake flour
½ teaspoon baking powder
⅛ teaspoon salt
¾ cup (1½ sticks) unsalted butter at room temperature
1 cup granulated sugar
3 large eggs
1 teaspoon vanilla extract
Chocolate Frosting or Chocolate Glaze (recipes follow)

Adjust a rack in the lower third of the oven. Preheat the oven to 350°F. Butter and flour two 6-inch round cake pans and knock out the excess flour.

Sift the flour, baking powder, and salt onto a sheet of waxed paper. In a large bowl, using an electric mixer on medium speed, cream the butter until soft and creamy. Add the sugar and continue beating until the mixture is light and fluffy. Beat in the eggs, one at a time. Add the vanilla. On low speed, gradually add the dry ingredients until thoroughly blended.

Spoon equal amounts of batter into each pan and smooth the tops evenly. Bake for about 30 minutes, or until light golden and the center of each cake springs back when lightly touched. Let the layers cool in the pans for 10 minutes, then unmold onto wire racks and let cool completely.

Frost or glaze to make one 2-layer American Baby Cake or two single-layer European Baby Cakes.

CHOCOLATE FROSTING FOR AMERICAN BABY CAKE
Makes 1 cup, enough for one 6-inch 2-layer cake

4 tablespoons unsalted butter
2 ounces unsweetened chocolate, chopped
2 cups confectioners' sugar
¼ cup milk
2 teaspoons vanilla extract

In a small, heavy saucepan, melt the butter and the chocolate over low heat. In a medium bowl, combine the confectioners' sugar with the milk and vanilla and stir until smooth. Add the chocolate mixture. Set the bowl over another bowl half-filled with ice water. With a rubber spatula, beat just until the frosting is thick enough to spread.

Spread one cake layer with about one-fourth of the frosting. Set the second layer on top and spread the remaining frosting on the sides and top of the cake. Using an icing spatula, make swirls on the top. Coat the sides with chopped nuts (see note).

CONTINUED

CHOCOLATE GLAZE FOR EUROPEAN BABY CAKES
This glaze is for 2 single-layer cakes. You can glaze both at the same time, or freeze one layer for another time. Set each cake on a wire rack over a baking sheet.

Makes ¾ cup, enough for two 6-inch single-layer cakes

4 ounces semisweet chocolate, finely chopped
½ cup heavy cream

Set the cake(s) on a wire rack over a baking sheet. Put the chocolate in a medium bowl. In a small saucepan, heat the cream just to a boil. Pour the cream over the chocolate. Whisk until the chocolate melts and the mixture is smooth and shiny.

Pour half the glaze over each cake to coat the top and sides. Set aside for about 30 minutes to let the glaze set before coating the sides with finely chopped nuts (see note).

If glazing only one cake, refrigerate the remaining glaze in an airtight container for up to 1 week (freeze the individual layers in an airtight wrap of plastic wrap and aluminum foil for up to 1 week). When ready to glaze the second cake, place the glaze in a double boiler over barely simmering water. Stir occasionally, just until the glaze is liquid again. Proceed to coat the cake as directed above.

NOTE: To decorate the sides of the cakes, you can coat them with chopped nuts. Here's a technique to make it easy: Pour the chopped nuts onto a baking sheet. With a metal spatula, lift the cake off its rack or plate and hold the cake in one hand directly over the nuts. Tilt the cake slightly and, with the other hand, gently press the nuts onto the frosting or glaze along the sides of the cake until they are covered. Press lightly with the clean blade of a flexible metal icing spatula to ensure that the nuts adhere neatly.

LAZY LADY CAKE

HERE'S THE NEXT-BEST THING TO MAKING YOUR OWN CAKE, FROM
LOUISE MOISES, A RARE-BOOK SELLER IN SAN FRANCISCO.
YOU COULD DO THE SAME THING WITH A BAKERY POUND CAKE,
SPONGE CAKE, OR GENOISE AND ALMOST ANY FROSTING
AND FILLING IN THIS BOOK.

*My specialty birthday cake is a "lazy lady" cake.
Since I don't have time to bake, I like to purchase the best angel food
cake, and then adapt it for the person celebrating.
I slice the cake into layers—four if possible—then add the filling:
bananas and whipped cream for Dad; strawberry jam
with whipped cream cheese filling, topped with fresh strawberries for
Mom; lemon filling and candied Meyer lemon slices, etc.*

—LOUISE MOISES

Green Cake (*Vert-vert*)

🎨

MARGUERITE, CLAUDE MONET'S COOK AT GIVERNY, MADE THIS EXOTIC CAKE
EVERY YEAR FOR HIS BIRTHDAY LUNCH ON NOVEMBER 14. FILLED WITH A PISTACHIO
CREAM, IT IS TOPPED WITH A LUMINOUS PALE GREEN FONDANT FROSTING.

MAKES ONE
8-INCH 3-LAYER
CAKE; SERVES
8 TO 10

SPINACH COLORING:
½ cup water
3 cups packed fresh spinach leaves

CAKE:
4 large eggs
¾ cup sugar
1 cup all-purpose flour, sifted
2 tablespoons ground pistachios
¼ cup kirsch
2 tablespoons unsalted butter at room
   temperature
Grated zest of 1 lemon

PISTACHIO CREAM:
¼ cup ground pistachios
2 tablespoons kirsch

2 cups plus 4 tablespoons (4½ sticks)
   unsalted butter at room temperature
2 teaspoons spinach coloring, above
⅓ cup sugar
2 large eggs
2 large egg yolks
2 teaspoons flour
1 cup milk

FONDANT FROSTING:
3 cups sugar
2 cups water
2 tablespoons white corn syrup
1 teaspoon spinach coloring, above
Juice of 1 lemon

MAKES ABOUT
1 CUP, ENOUGH
TO FROST 1 CAKE

To make the spinach coloring: Bring the water to a boil in a medium saucepan, add the spinach, cover, and cook for 1 minute. Transfer the liquid and spinach to a sieve set over a bowl and press the spinach through the sieve using the back of a large spoon. This will make a green purée to color the pistachio cream and the frosting.

To make the cake: Preheat the oven to 300°F. Butter an 8-inch cake pan.

In a medium saucepan, combine the eggs and sugar. Place the pan over low heat and beat the mixture until it has doubled in volume. Gradually beat in the flour until completely incorporated. Add the pistachios, kirsch, butter, and lemon zest. Stir well until blended.

Pour the batter into the prepared pan and bake for 30 minutes, or until a cake tester or toothpick inserted in the center comes out clean. Remove from the oven and invert the pan onto a wire rack; let cool completely.

To make the pistachio cream: Combine the pistachios, kirsch, and 2 tablespoons of the butter in a small bowl. Stir to make a paste. Stir in the spinach coloring. In a medium saucepan, combine the sugar, eggs, and egg yolks. Beat in the flour and milk. Place the pan over low heat

and beat in the pistachio mixture. Remove from heat and beat in the remaining 2 cups plus 2 tablespoons butter.

Carefully slice the cake into 3 equal layers. Spread each of 2 rounds with half of the pistachio cream. Stack the layers, topping with the third layer. Refrigerate.

To make the fondant frosting: Combine the sugar and water in a medium, heavy saucepan. Place over high heat and cook, without stirring, until the sugar dissolves and the mixture begins to boil. Cook to the large-thread stage (that is, when a little of the syrup dropped into cold water forms a large thread). Stir in the corn syrup and spinach coloring. Remove from heat.

Lightly oil a marble work surface (see note). Pour the syrup onto the surface and work it with a wooden spatula until it starts to become opaque. Sprinkle with the lemon juice and continue working until it is a smooth, pale green paste. Roll into a ball and wrap in a damp cloth. Cover and refrigerate until needed. Roll it out with a rolling pin and use it to cover the cake.

OUR NOTE: If you don't have a marble work surface, use a heavy baking sheet.

Bittersweet Chocolate Pinwheel Cake

❧

THIS SOPHISTICATED DOUBLE-CHOCOLATE CAKE, A PERFECT BIRTHDAY CAKE FOR
TRUE CHOCOLATE-LOVERS, IS FROM CARRIE BROWN, CHEF/OWNER OF
THE JIMTOWN STORE NEAR HEALDSBURG, CALIFORNIA. THE RECIPE, ALONG WITH MANY
OTHER BROWN FAMILY FAVORITES, IS FROM CARRIE'S BOOK,
THE JIMTOWN STORE COOKBOOK. SHE ADAPTED IT FROM THE RECIPE HER MOTHER
USED FOR FAMILY BIRTHDAY CAKES WHEN CARRIE WAS GROWING UP.

The beauty of this extraordinary cake is the blending in each bite of the pure essence of unsweetened chocolate in the pinwheel with the slightly sweetened chocolate in the cake. It's an unusual and indulgent tasting experience. Serve with a small scoop of vanilla ice cream, if you please.

—CARRIE BROWN

MAKES ONE
9-INCH 4-LAYER
CAKE; SERVES 8

4 ounces top-quality unsweetened chocolate, such as Scharffen Berger, chopped

1¾ cups sifted cake flour, measured by spoon and sweep (see page 17)

1½ cups granulated sugar

2 teaspoons baking powder

¼ teaspoon baking soda

1 teaspoon salt

½ cup (1 stick) unsalted butter at room temperature

1 cup heavy cream

1 teaspoon vanilla extract

2 large eggs at room temperature

¼ cup milk

FLUFFY CHOCOLATE FILLING:

2 ounces top-quality unsweetened chocolate, such as Scharffen Berger, chopped

1½ cups (3 sticks) unsalted butter at room temperature

1 cup confectioners' sugar

⅔ cup heavy cream

2 tablespoons brandy

1 teaspoon vanilla extract

¼ teaspoon salt

Position a rack in the middle of the oven. Preheat the oven to 350°F. Butter two 9-inch round cake pans. Line the bottom of each pan with a round of parchment paper or waxed paper. Butter the paper. Dust the bottom and sides of the pans with flour and tap out the excess. If your kitchen is particularly warm, refrigerate the pans while making the batter.

First, make the cake: In a double boiler over barely simmering water, melt 2 ounces of the chocolate. Remove from heat.

Sift the flour, sugar, baking powder, baking soda, and salt together onto a sheet of waxed paper.

In a large bowl, using an electric mixer on medium speed, beat the butter until smooth. Add the cream, the dry ingredients, and the vanilla. On low speed, beat until incorporated. Continue to beat for 2 minutes, scraping down the sides of the bowl once or twice. Add the eggs, milk, and melted chocolate and continue to beat for 1 minute. Evenly divide the batter between the prepared pans. Set aside.

In a double boiler over barely simmering water, melt the remaining 2 ounces chocolate. Remove from heat and let cool slightly. Drizzle half the chocolate over the batter in each of the pans in a circle about 1 inch in from the edge. With a small rubber spatula, swirl the chocolate as if tracing a ring of cursive lowercase e's; this is the pinwheel.

CONTINUED

Bake for about 30 minutes, or until the cake layers begin to pull away from the sides of the pans and the tops spring back when gently pressed with a finger. (You will also notice a wonderful chocolate fragrance when the layers are almost done.)

Transfer the pans to wire racks and let the cakes cool for 10 minutes. Run a sharp knife around the sides of each and invert onto the wire racks. Immediately turn the layers right side up on the racks and let cool to room temperature.

To make the filling: In the top of a double boiler over simmering water, melt the chocolate. As it melts, stir with a spoon. When smooth, remove from the heat and let cool slightly.

In a medium bowl, cream the butter with an electric handheld mixer set on high until smooth. Add the sugar and beat until light and fluffy. Add the cream, chocolate, brandy, vanilla, and salt and beat until incorporated.

With a long, serrated knife, split each cake layer in half horizontally. Select the top layer with the most attractive pinwheel and set it aside. Set the other top layer, pinwheel down, on a cake plate. Cover the layer with one-third of the filling, spreading it to the edges. Repeat with the second and third layers. Top with the reserved top layer, pinwheel side up.

Refrigerate for at least 1 hour or as long as overnight before serving. Cut into wedges and serve cold. Store any leftover cake by first pressing a square of parchment paper or waxed paper against the cut sides of the cake, then wrapping the entire cake in plastic wrap and refrigerating it.

A Birthday Surprise

Lady Caroline Lamb (1785–1828), the wife of the English prime minister Lord Melbourne, was known for her flamboyance. She may have started a new tradition on one of her husband's birthdays, when she arranged to have herself served to him at a birthday banquet in a very large tureen, from which she emerged in the nude.

Birthday Cupcakes

CHILDREN ADORE CUPCAKES, WHICH MAKES THEM A DELIGHTFUL CHOICE FOR A CHILD'S
BIRTHDAY PARTY: THEY'RE EASY FOR THE COOK TO MAKE AND TO SERVE,
AND EACH CHILD CAN HAVE HIS OR HER OWN LITTLE CAKE, TOPPED WITH A CANDLE.
ADULTS AS WELL AS KIDS WILL LOVE THESE CHOCOLATE CUPCAKES;
ADAPTED FROM A RECIPE BY FOOD STYLIST STEPHANIE GREENLEIGH, THEY SPORT A
SEVEN-MINUTE FROSTING SPRINKLED WITH CRUSHED PEPPERMINT CANDIES.

MAKES 12
CUPCAKES

1½ cups cake flour
1½ cups sugar
1 teaspoon baking soda
¼ teaspoon baking powder
½ teaspoon salt
½ cup unsweetened cocoa powder
1 cup warm water
2 large eggs at room temperature
½ cup vegetable oil
1 teaspoon vanilla extract
¾ cup mint chocolate chips

FLUFFY FROSTING
¾ cup sugar
3 large egg whites
⅓ cup light corn syrup
⅛ teaspoon salt
1 teaspoon peppermint extract
2 drops red food coloring (optional)

4 ounces peppermint candies, crushed

MAKES ENOUGH
TO FROST 12
CUPCAKES

Preheat the oven to 350°F. Line 12 muffin cups with paper liners.

In a large bowl, whisk the cake flour, sugar, baking soda, baking powder, and salt together to blend, and set aside.

Dissolve the cocoa in the warm water. Beat in the eggs, oil, and vanilla by hand until well combined. Gradually beat in the dry ingredients just until the batter is evenly mixed. Fold in the mint chocolate chips.

Spoon the batter into the paper liners, filling them three-fourths full. Bake until a toothpick inserted in the center of a cupcake comes out clean, 25 to 30 minutes. Transfer the cupcakes to wire racks and let them cool completely.

To make the frosting: In a double boiler, combine the sugar, egg whites, corn syrup, and salt over low heat. Beat with an electric mixer on medium speed until stiff peaks form, about 7 minutes. Remove from the heat and stir in the peppermint extract and red food coloring, if using, blending well to distribute the color. Let the frosting cool completely.

Frost the cupcakes with the frosting and sprinkle with the crushed peppermint candies.

Buttermilk Poppy Seed Bundt Cake

CHEF AND RESTAURATEUR CINDY PAWLCYN GAINED AN INSTANT FAMILY
WHEN SHE MARRIED A SCOTSMAN WITH TWO CHILDREN, AND THE CHILDREN GAINED NOT
JUST A STEPMOTHER BUT ALSO A FAMILY TRADITION OF AMERICAN BIRTHDAY CAKES—
SPECIFICALLY THIS BUNDT CAKE FROM CINDY'S MOTHER, DOROTHY PAWLCYN.

I always make (when time and her location allow) a poppy seed cake for my stepdaughter Kirstie's birthday. It all started the first summer after Murdo and I got married. We (the Pawlcyns) had always gone on a summer trip, so I did the same with my new family: my husband, Murdo, and his children, Kirstie and Peter. I think the kids were nine and eleven at the time.

My mom, being an ultimate mom/gram/stepgram, kept us busy and made the kids feel right at home. They had long been part of a single-parent, nonfood, nonextended family (all of their relatives are in Scotland). My mom's good Midwestern tradition provided us with cookies, an overflowing icebox, a huge bowl of M&M's (a tradition dating back to my gram), lots of Cokes, 7-Ups, orange pop, potato chips, and cake—buttermilk poppy seed Bundt cake.

The kids woke up the first morning to crepes and the second morning to waffles, and promptly informed me that they were not ever going to leave.

Needless to say, the next December when I asked Kirstie what she wanted for a birthday cake, she looked at me as though I were mad and said, "The poppy seed one from your mom, what else?"

—CINDY PAWLCYN

4 tablespoons poppy seeds
1 cup buttermilk
1 cup (2 sticks) unsalted butter at
    room temperature
1½ cups granulated sugar
4 large eggs, separated, at room tem-
    perature
1 teaspoon almond extract
2 teaspoons grated lemon or orange
    zest
2½ cups all-purpose flour
1 teaspoon baking soda
2 teaspoons baking powder
½ teaspoon salt

LEMON OR ORANGE ICING:
2 cups confectioners' sugar, sifted
Grated zest and juice of 2 lemons or
    oranges
Heavy cream as needed

In a small bowl, combine the poppy seeds and butter-milk. Let sit for 1 hour.

Preheat the oven to 350°F. Butter and flour a 10-cup Bundt pan (even if it is nonstick).

In a large bowl, cream the butter and 1 cup of the granulated sugar together until light and fluffy. Beat in the egg yolks and the almond extract. Stir in the lemon or orange zest.

Sift the flour, baking soda, baking powder, and salt together onto a piece of waxed paper. Stir the dry ingredients into the butter mixture alternately with the buttermilk mixture until smooth.

In a large bowl, beat the egg whites until soft peaks form. Gradually beat in the remaining ½ cup sugar and continue beating until stiff, glossy peaks form. Fold the whites into the batter by thirds; the batter will be very stiff.

Pour the batter into the prepared pan and smooth the top. Bake in the oven for 45 minutes, or until a toothpick inserted in the center comes out clean. Cool for 10 minutes in the pan; turn out onto a cooling rack.

To make the icing: Put the confectioners' sugar into a large bowl and add the zest and juice. Stir to blend, adding heavy cream as needed for a pourable consistency. Spread the icing over the cake.

12
BIRTHDAY CANDLES

by
Betty Bolling

BAKING EQUIPMENT AND
CAKE-DECORATING SUPPLIES

Most of the pans and decorating supplies called for in
this book are available at kitchenware stores, but you
can also order them by mail, phone, or online.

The Baker's Catalogue
P.O. Box 876
Norwich, VT 05055
800-827-6836
www.bakerscatalogue.com
Baking pans, equipment, flours, sugars, and special
ingredients from the King Arthur Flour company.

Bridge Kitchenware
214 East 52nd Street
New York, NY 10022
212-688-4220
www.bridgekitchenware.com
Cake pans and kitchen utensils.

Cake Art
1512 Fifth Avenue
San Rafael, CA 94901
415-456-7773
www.cakeartsupplies.com
Wilton cake-decorating supplies, including cake toppers.

Chef's Tool Box
6020 Dillard Circle
Austin, TX 78752
512-467-1994/877-345-CHEF (2433)
www.chefsupply.com
Ateco pastry bags.

Cook's Dream, Inc.
8123 East Sprague
Spokane, WA 99212
509-536-0166/866-285-COOK (2665)
www.ultimatebaker.com
A wide variety of cake supplies.

India Tree
4240 Gilman Place West, No. B
Seattle, WA 98199
206-270-0293/800-369-4848
www.indiatree.com
Candied violets and rose petals, silver dragées.

Martha Stewart: The Catalog for Living
P.O. Box 11650
Pueblo, CO 81001
800-950-7130
www.marthastewart.com
Cake-decorating kits, stencils, and food coloring.

Michaele Thunen Designs
63 Northampton Avenue
Berkeley, CA 94707
510-527-5279
www.michaelethunen.com
Party favors, mementos.

New York Cake and Baking Supply
56 West 22nd Street
New York, NY 10010
212-675-2253/800-942-2539
www.nycake.com
Kitchen equipment and special ingredients.

Nordic Ware
Highways 7 and 100
Minneapolis, MN 55416
952-920-2888/800-328-4310
www.nordicware.com
Bundt pans and aluminum bakeware.

Pastry Chef Central
1355 West Palmetto Park Road, Suite 302
Boca Raton, FL 33486
561-999-9483
www.pastrychef.com
Pastry tools and bakeware.

Patty Cakes
34-55 Junction Boulevard
Jackson Heights, NY 11372
718-651-5770
www.pattycakes.com
Ateco cake-decorating kits.

Penzeys, Ltd.
P.O. Box 933
Muskego, WI 53150
800-741-7787
www.penzeys.com
A wide array of spices and flavorings.

Sugarcraft
2715 Dixie Highway
Hamilton, OH 45015
513-896-7089
www.sugarcraft.com
Doll picks and other decorating supplies.

Sur La Table
Catalog Division
1765 Sixth Avenue South
Seattle, WA 98134
800-243-0852
www.surlatable.com
Baking utensils of all kinds. Ask for the "Tools of the Cook" catalogue.

Sweet Celebrations
P.O. Box 39426
Edina, MN 55436
800-328-6722
www.sweetc.com
A wide variety of cake-baking equipment, including pastry bags and tips. (Formerly called Maid of Scandinavia.)

Williams-Sonoma
P.O. Box 7456
San Francisco, CA 94120
800-541-2233
www.williams-sonoma.com
Baking pans and tools, plus baking ingredients such as high-quality vanilla.

Wilton Industries
2240 West 75th Street
Woodridge, IL 60517
800-794-5866
www.wilton.com
Cake pans and cake-decorating supplies, including paste coloring.

Props courtesy of: Toni Elling, Meadowsweets, Middleburgh, New York; Jennifer Davis, Prize in San Francisco; Alice Erb and Lauren McIntosh, Tail of the Yak, Berkeley, California; Wendy Addison, Theatre of Dreams, Port Costa, California; Julie Hellwich, Girl Babies; Elizabeth DeScala, Buttons and Bows, San Anselmo, California; Ada Fitzman, The Paper Pile, San Anselmo, California; Barbara Markle, Pink Geranium, San Anselmo, California; Michelle and Carolyn Charton, Columbine, Corte Madera, California; Main Street Floragardens, San Anselmo, California.

White Mountain Cake: From *James Beard's American Cookery* by James Beard. Copyright © 1972 by James Beard (text); copyright © 1972 by Little, Brown and Company (illustrations). By permission of Little, Brown and Company (Inc.).

Orange Chiffon Cake and Carrot Cake: From *Maida Heatter's Cakes* by Maida Heatter. Copyright © 1982, 1985, and 1997 by Maida Heatter. Reprinted by permission of Cader Books.

Gingerbread Cake with Chocolate Icing: From *Home Cooking: A Writer in the Kitchen* by Laurie Colwin, copyright © 1988 by Laurie Colwin. Used by permission of Alfred A. Knopf, a division of Random House, Inc.

Aunt Frances's Ricotta Cheesecake: courtesy of Donata Maggipinto.

Heavenly Angel Cake: From *San Francisco Chronicle Cookbook* by Michael Bauer and Fran Irwin, eds. © 1997. Published by Chronicle Books LLC, San Francisco. Used with permission.

Cocoa Whipped Cream Frosting: courtesy of Eloise Kleinman.

Frying Pan Chocolate Cake: courtesy of Georgeanne Brennan.

Jelly Roll: From *Sugar Pie and Jelly Roll* by Robbin Gourley. Copyright © 2000 by the author. Reprinted by permission of Algonquin Books of Chapel Hill, a division of Workman Publishing.

German Chocolate Cake: From *The New Southern Cook* by John Martin Taylor, copyright © 1995 by John Martin Taylor. Used by permission of Bantam Books, a division of Random House, Inc.

1-2-3-4 Cake: From *Fanny at Chez Panisse* by Alice Waters and Bob Carrau and Patricia Curtan and illustrated by Ann Arnold. Copyright © 1992 by Tango Rose, Inc. Reprinted by permission of HarperCollins Publishers Inc.

Fastest Fudge Cake: From *A Year in Chocolate* by Alice Medrich. Copyright © 2001 by Alice Medrich. By permission of Warner Books, Inc.

Becky's Birthday Cake: From *The Tasha Tudor Cookbook* by Tasha Tudor. Copyright © 1993 by Tasha Tudor. By permission of Little, Brown and Company, Inc.

Paw Paw's Birthday Caramel Cake with Caramel Frosting: From *My Mother's Southern Desserts* by James Villas. Copyright © 1998 by James Villas. Reprinted by permission of HarperCollins Publishers Inc.

Grandmothers' Chocolate Cake: courtesy of Emily Luchetti.

Benoît's Upside-Down Caramelized Apple Tart and Flaky Pastry: From *The Paris Cookbook* by Patricia Wells. Copyright © 2001 by Patricia Wells. Reprinted by permission of HarperCollins Publishers Inc.

Grandmother Whitehead's Famous Texas Fudge Cake: The recipe for Texas Fudge Cake and the story "The Best Birthday" are reprinted from *Chicken Soup for the Soul Cookbook* by Mary Olsen Kelly, with permission of Health Communications, Inc.

Princess Cake: Reprinted with permission from *The Village Baker's Wife* by Gayle and Joe Ortiz. Copyright © 1997 by Gayle Ortiz, Joe Ortiz, and Louisa Beers, Ten Speed Press, Berkeley, CA. Available by visiting us online at www.tenspeed.com.

Old-Fashioned Banana Spice Cake: From *Breakfast, Lunch & Dinner* by Bradley Ogden, copyright © 1991 by Bradley Ogden. Used by permission of Random House, Inc.

Le Kilimanjaro—Glace au Chocolat, Pralinée: From *Mastering the Art of French Cooking* by Julia Child and Simone Beck, copyright © 1961 by Alfred A. Knopf, a division of Random House, Inc. Used by permission of Alfred A. Knopf, a division of Random House, Inc.

Meyer Lemon Pound Cake and Birthday Cupcakes: Reprinted with permission from *Baked from the Heart* by Stephanie Greenleigh, Kathryn Kleinman, and Jennifer Barry. Copyright © 1997 by Stephanie Greenleigh, Ten Speed Press, Berkeley, CA. Birthday Cupcakes recipe was originally published under the name "Royal Hearts Cupcakes" on page 46. Available by visiting us online at www.tenspeed.com.

Bauer, Michael, and Fran Irwin, eds. *The San Francisco Chronicle Cookbook*. San Francisco: Chronicle Books, 1997.

Beard, James. *James Beard's American Cookery*. Boston: Little, Brown and Company, 1972.

Braker, Flo. *The Simple Art of Perfect Baking*. New York: William Morrow and Company, 1984.

Brody, Lora. *Basic Baking*. New York: HarperCollins, 2000.

Canfield, Jack, et al. *Chicken Soup for the Soul: 101 Stories with Recipes from the Heart*. Rev. ed. Deerfield Beach, Fla.: Health Communications, 1995.

Child, Julia, and Simone Beck. *Mastering the Art of French Cooking, Vol. 2*. New York: Alfred A. Knopf, 1970.

Colwin, Laurie. *Home Cooking: A Writer in the Kitchen*. New York: HarperPerennial, 1993.

Cook's Illustrated, June 2002, no. 56, pp. 24–25.

Cunningham, Marion. *The Fannie Farmer Cookbook*. New York: Alfred A. Knopf, 1996.

Fisher, M. F. K. *With Bold Knife and Fork*. 1969. Reprint, New York: Counterpoint, 2002.

Fitch, Noël Riley. *Appetite for Life: The Biography of Julia Child*. New York: Doubleday, 1997.

Fobel, Jim. *Jim Fobel's Old-Fashioned Baking Book: Recipes from an American Childhood*. New York: Lake Isle Press, 1996.

Gourley, Robbin. *Sugar Pie and Jelly Roll: Sweets from a Southern Kitchen*. New York: Workman Publishing, 2000.

Greenleigh, Stephanie, et al. *Baked from the Heart*. Berkeley, Calif.: Ten Speed Press, 1997.

Heatter, Maida. *Maida Heatter's Cakes*. New York: Cader Books, 1997.

Joyes, Claire. *Monet's Table: The Cooking Journals of Claude Monet*. New York: Simon & Schuster, 1989.

Lewis, Linda Rannells. *Birthdays: Their Delights & Disappointments, Past & Present, Worldly, Astrological, & Infamous*. Boston: Little, Brown and Company, 1976.

Luchetti, Emily. *Stars Desserts*. New York: HarperCollins, 1991.

Medrich, Alice. *A Year in Chocolate: Four Seasons of Unforgettable Desserts*. New York: Warner Books, 2001.

Ogden, Bradley. *Bradley Ogden's Breakfast, Lunch & Dinner: Savory American Fare for Contemporary Cooks*. New York: Random House, 1991.

Ortiz, Gayle and Joe Ortiz. *The Village Baker's Wife: The Desserts and Pastries That Made Gayle's Famous*. Berkeley, Calif.: Ten Speed Press, 1997.

Perl, Lila. *Candles, Cakes, and Donkey Tails: Birthday Symbols and Celebrations*. New York: Clarion Books, 1984.

Pollan, Michael. *The Botany of Desire: A Plant's-Eye View of the World*. New York: Random House, 2001.

Rodgers, Rick, ed. *The Baker's Dozen Cookbook*. New York: HarperCollins, 2001.

Sanchez, Maria Bruscino. *Sweet Maria's Cake Kitchen: Casual and Creative Recipes for Layer, Loaf, and Bundt Cakes*. New York: St. Martin's Press, 1998.

Taylor, John Martin. *The New Southern Cook: 2000 Recipes from the South's Best Chefs and Home Cooks*. New York: Bantam Books, 1995.

Tudor, Tasha. *The Tasha Tudor Cookbook: Recipes and Reminiscences from Corgi Cottage*. New York: Little, Brown and Company, 1993.

Villas, James. *My Mother's Southern Desserts: More Than 180 Treasured Family Recipes for Holiday and Everyday Celebrations*. New York: William Morrow and Company, 1998.

Waters, Alice. *Chez Panisse Café Cookbook*. New York: HarperCollins, 1999.

———. *Fanny at Chez Panisse: A Child's Restaurant Adventures, with 46 Recipes*. New York: HarperCollins, 1992.

Wells, Patricia. *The Paris Cookbook*. New York: HarperCollins, 2001.

ACKNOWLEDGMENTS

Like a many-layered birthday cake, this book was created with inspiration, work, and love. It would not have been possible without the help of many talented and generous people. The bakers, friends, and family members whose recipes, stories, and wisdom are included in these pages have given me the opportunity to make my wish—this book—come true. ◆ Many thanks to: my mom, Eloise Kleinman, for her constant love and support, and for passing on to me the love of family, tradition, and sugar: the ingredients that made this book possible. Her many birthday cakes for our family gave me the vision to dream about this project. ◆ Carolyn Miller, my text writer, for her support and guidance with the words and recipes in this book. Her love of baking and sharing birthday cakes helped to give my idea a voice and bring the message of this book to life. ◆ Michael Mabry, my designer, and his staff, Sarah Keith, Margie Chu, and Peter Soe, for their wonderful support and talent. ◆ Stephanie Greenleigh, food stylist extraordinaire, for her birthday recipes and fabulous cake baking and styling, and Debbie Birrell, Amanda Marcus, Claudia Breault, and Teresa Retzlaff, for their valuable help baking, testing recipes, and assisting Stephanie and me throughout this project. ◆ Chronicle Books and Leslie Jonath, my editor at Chronicle Books, for believing in this project and supporting me throughout the long process of making a book, and to Laurel Mainard, Leslie's assistant, for her focus and clarity. Thanks also to designers Vivien Sung and Ben Shaykin at Chronicle, and copyeditor Sharilyn Hovind, for their assistance and support. ◆ Patricia Wilson of the Make-a-Wish Foundation for her excitement and enthusiasm for this project. Patricia's steadfast support made our connection with MAW possible. And thanks to Steve Miller and Laura Hopkins for opening the doors to begin the process of working with the Make-a-Wish Foundation. ◆ Teresa Retzlaff, my studio manager. Without her relentless search for birthday cake recipes and stories, I would have been overwhelmed by the daunting task of turning my idea for this book into a reality. ◆ Shashona Burke, my studio manager, for her patience and skill at keeping me organized and taking on many of the tedious details of finishing this book after Teresa began her new life in Oregon. ◆ Brad Bunnin, my legal council, for his sensibility and fairness in making sure this book became the gift that I wanted it to be. ◆ Kirstie Tweed, Anthony Gamboa, and Yael Dahan, my photo assistants, for keeping my photography job fun and focused, and Jessica Haye, Carol Rossi, and Michael Lamotte, for their finely tuned tech support. ◆ My caring friends and family, for donating their special birthday cake memorabilia: Sara Slavin, Michaele Thunen, Amanda Marcus, Amy Tan, Carrie Brown, Rosie Robertson, Karen Kleinman Knaeble, Barbara Jucick Kleinman, Jim Kleinman, and Gala Holton. A special thank-you to Jeff Marcus for lending me his mom's charming recipe book. ◆ My dear friends, for their support of this project: Amanda Marcus, Amy Tan, Donata Maggipinto, Jill Lurue Rieser, Nancy Green, Susan Watkins, Carrie Brown, Janet Tokerud, Tori Richie, Jackie Jones, Amy Nathan, Mary Hardy, and all of my garage workout queens. My treasured friend, Sara Slavin—my angel in the wings—for keeping my vision clear and listening to my thoughts on our early-morning walks. And to my husband, Michael Schwab, and my sons, Eric and Peter, for continuing to put up with my intensity during the many stages of making this book. ◆ Finally, my heartfelt thanks and appreciation to Michael Mabry, esteemed designer, for his elegant vision, graphic style, and whimsical book design—his work is the icing on the cake.

 My thanks to these celebrated bakers and storytellers for their recipes and words: James Beard (1903–85), Louisa Beers, Flo Braker, Georgeanne Brennan, Carrie Brown, Julia Child, Laurie Colwin (1944–92), Marion Cunningham, Catherine Cunningham, Editors of *Cooks Illustrated*, Elizabeth Falkner, Sherry Falkner, M. F. K. Fisher (1908–92), Noël Riley Fitch, Jim Fobel, Sam Godfrey, Debbie Jensen Gonnet, Henry Gonnet, Robbin Gourley, Stephanie Greenleigh, Maida Heatter, Mary Olsen Kelly, Patricia Kislevitz, Eloise Kleinman, David Lebovitz, Emily Luchetti, Donata Maggipinto, Amy Mai, Alice Medrich, Carolyn Miller, Glenn and Laura Miwa, Louise Moises, Bradley Ogden, Gayle Ortiz, Cindy Pawlcyn, Dorothy Pawlcyn, Michael Pollan, Teresa Retzlaff, Maria Bruscino Sanchez, Richard Sax (1949–95), Wendy Schubring, Beth Setrakian, Lindsey Shere, Kathleen Stewart, Hannah Tai, Amy Tan, John Martin Taylor, Tasha Tudor, James Villas, Martha Pearl Villas, Alice Waters, Fanny Singer, Patricia Wells, and Chuck Williams.

JANUARY

FEBRUARY

MARCH

APRIL

MAY

JUNE

JULY

AUGUST

SEPTEMBER

OCTOBER

NOVEMBER

DECEMBER

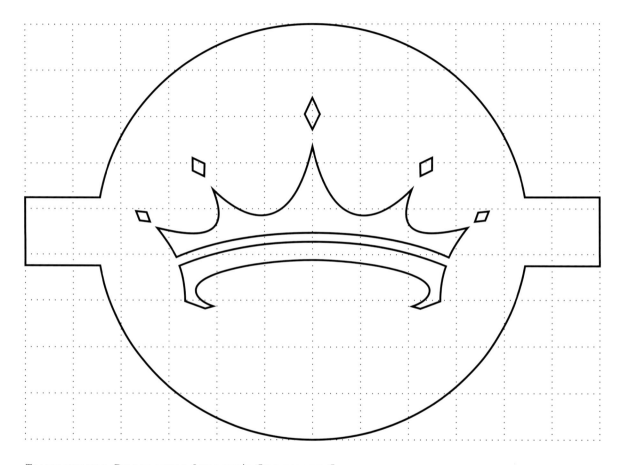

TEMPLATE FOR DECORATING LINDSEY'S CHOCOLATE CAKE
WITH CONFECTIONER'S SUGAR
Enlarge 200 percent, to a 9-inch diameter circle.
Each square equals 1 inch.

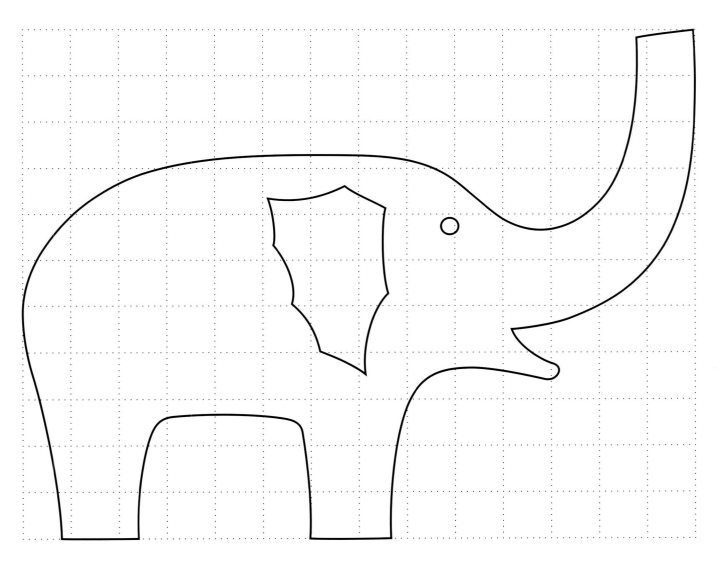

TEMPLATE FOR PINK ELEPHANT CUTOUT CAKE
Enlarge 200 percent, to 11 by 14 inches.
Each square equals 1 inch.

Angel Cake, Heavenly, 39
Apple Tart, Benoît's Upside-Down Caramelized, 63–64
Aunt Frances's Ricotta Cheesecake, 36

Baby Cakes, 113–114
Banana Spice Cake, Old-Fashioned, 74
Becky's Birthday Cake, 56–57
Benoît's Upside-Down Caramelized Apple Tart, 63–64
Beth's Very Berry Shortcake, 101
Birthday cakes
    baking tips, 13
    decorating and serving tips, 21–25
    equipment, 15–16
    ingredients, 14
    sources for supplies, 127–128
    symbolism, 10, 73
    techniques, 17–18
Birthday Cupcakes, 122
Bittersweet Chocolate Frosting, 60
Bittersweet Chocolate Pinwheel Cake, 119–120
Boiled White Frosting, 57
Bundt Cake, Buttermilk Poppy Seed, 124–125
Buttercream
    Buttercream Frosting, 98
        for 1-2-3-4 Cupcakes, 52
    Orange Buttercream Frosting, 32
Buttermilk Poppy Seed Bundt Cake, 124–125

Caramel
    Benoît's Upside-Down Caramelized Apple Tart, 63–64
    Caramel Sauce, 93
    Paw Paw's Birthday Caramel Cake with Caramel
        Frosting, 58
Carrot Cake, 43–44
Cheese
    Aunt Frances's Ricotta Cheesecake, 36
    Cream Cheese and Coconut Frosting, 82
    Cream Cheese Icing, 43–44

Chocolate
    curls, to make, 23
    to melt, 17
Chocolate cakes
    Birthday Cupcakes, 122
    Bittersweet Chocolate Pinwheel Cake, 119–120
    Easiest Hot Fudge Pudding Cake, 110–111
    The Elvis Cake, 95
    Fastest Fudge Cake, 54–55
    Frying Pan Chocolate Cake, 40–41
    German Chocolate Cake, 49
    Grandmothers' Chocolate Cake, 60
    Grandmother Whitehead's Famous Texas Fudge
        Cake, 66–67
    Le Kilimanjaro — Glace au Chocolat, Pralinée, 76–77
    Lindsey's Chocolate Cake, 87
Chocolate frostings and icings
    Bittersweet Chocolate Frosting, 60
    Chocolate Frosting for American Baby Cake, 113
    Chocolate Ganache, 105
    Chocolate Glaze for European Baby Cakes, 114
    Chocolate Icing, 35
    Cocoa Whipped Cream Frosting, 39
        for Cream Puffs (variation), 93
    Fast Fudge Frosting, 55
        as sauce for Cream Puffs (variation), 93
    Grandma's Fudge Frosting, 81
    Grandmother Whitehead's Famous Texas Fudge
        Cake Icing, 67
Chocolate Ice Cream, 77
Cocoa Whipped Cream Frosting
    for Cream Puffs (variation), 93
Coconut
    Comforts Coconut Cake with Cream Cheese and
        Coconut Frosting, 82–84
    in German Chocolate Cake Icing, 49
    to toast and tint, 23
    in White Mountain Cake, 29
Comforts Coconut Cake with Cream Cheese and
    Coconut Frosting, 82–84
Cream, whipped. See Whipped cream

Cream cheese
    Cream Cheese and Coconut Frosting, 82
    Cream Cheese Icing, 43–44
Cream Puffs with Lemon Filling, 90–93
Cupcakes
    Birthday Cupcakes, 122
    Comforts Coconut Cupcakes, 84
    1-2-3-4 Cupcakes, 52
Custard filling for Old-Fashioned Banana Spice Cake, 74

decorating and serving
    glossary and suggestions, 23–25
    sources for supplies, 127–128
    templates, 138–139
    tips, 21, 70, 84, 98
    tools, 22

Easiest Hot Fudge Pudding Cake, 110–111
Eggs
    separating and beating, 18
    tips for baking with, 13, 14
The Elvis Cake, 95
equipment
    basic, 15–16
    sources, 127–128

Fallen-Soufflé Cake (Lindsey's Chocolate Cake), 87
Fastest Fudge Cake, 54–55
Fast Fudge Frosting, 55
    as sauce for Cream Puffs (variation), 93
Fillings
    Berry Filling and Topping, 101
    custard for Old-Fashioned Banana Spice Cake, 74
    Fluffy Chocolate Filling, 119
    Lemon Curd, 92
    Lincoln Log Cake whipped cream filling (substitution),
        105
    Pastry Cream, 71
        for Cream Puffs (variation), 93
    Pistachio Cream, 117

Flavored Whipped Cream, 68, 101
Fluffy Chocolate Filling, 119
Fluffy Frosting, 122
    for Pink Elephant Cutout Cake, 108
Fondant Frosting, 117
Frostings and icings
    Bittersweet Chocolate Frosting, 60
    Boiled White Frosting, 57
    Buttercream Frosting, 98
        for 1-2-3-4 Cupcakes, 52
    Caramel Frosting, 58
    Chocolate Frosting for American Baby Cake, 113
    Chocolate Ganache, 105
    Chocolate Glaze for European Baby Cakes, 114
    Chocolate Icing, 35
    Cocoa Whipped Cream Frosting, 39
        for Cream Puffs (variation), 93
    Cream Cheese and Coconut Frosting, 82
    Cream Cheese Icing, 43
    Fast Fudge Frosting, 55
        as sauce for Cream Puffs (variation), 93
    Flavored Whipped Cream, 68, 101
    Fluffy Frosting, 122
        for Pink Elephant Cutout Cake, 108
    Fondant Frosting, 117
    German Chocolate Cake Icing, 49
    Grandma's Fudge Frosting, 81
    Grandmother Whitehead's Famous Texas Fudge
        Cake Icing, 67
    Lemon Icing, for Gingerbread Cake (variation), 35
    Lemon or Orange Icing, 125
    Orange Buttercream Frosting, 32
    Penuche Frosting, 97
    Seven-Minute Frosting, 29
    Seven-Minute Frosting (Fluffy Frosting), 122
    Whipped Cream Frosting, 95
        for Cream Puffs (variation), 93
        for Jelly Roll, 46
        for Orange Chiffon Cake (variation), 32
        for Pineapple Upside-Down Cake, 102

Fruit
 Benoît's Upside-Down Caramelized Apple Tart, 63–64
 Beth's Very Berry Shortcake, 101
 Carrot Cake, raisins in, 43–44
 The Elvis Cake, bananas in, 95
 Lemon Curd, 92
  for 1-2-3-4 Cake, 50–52
  for Comforts Coconut Cake with Cream Cheese and
   Coconut Frosting (variation), 84
 Lemon Filling, 90–92
 Lemon Icing, for Gingerbread Cake (variation), 35
 Lemon or Orange Icing, 125
 Meyer Lemon Pound Cake, 79
 Old-Fashioned Banana Spice Cake, 74
 Orange Chiffon Cake, 31–32
 Pavlova, mixed fruit in, 88–89
 Pineapple Upside-Down Cake (option and variations),
  102–103
Frying Pan Chocolate Cake, 40–41
Fudge Cake, Fastest, 54–55

Ganache, Chocolate, 105–106
Genoise Layer Cake, Vanilla, 68
German Chocolate Cake, 49
Gingerbread Cake with Chocolate Icing, 34–35
Glace au Chocolat, Pralinée — Le Kilimanjaro, 77
Glaze, Chocolate, 114
Gold Cake with Grandma's Fudge Frosting, 80–81
Grandmothers' Chocolate Cake, 60
Grandmother Whitehead's Famous Texas Fudge Cake,
 66–67
Green Cake (Vert-vert), 117

Heavenly Angel Cake, 39

Ice cream
 Chocolate Ice Cream, 77
 for Cream Puffs (variation), 93
 for Lincoln Log Cake, 105–106
Icings. See Frostings and icings
ingredients, basic, 14

Jelly Roll, 46

Lazy Lady Cake, 115
Le Kilimanjaro — Glace au Chocolat, Pralinée, 76–77
Lemon
 Lemon Curd, 92
  for 1-2-3-4 Cake (option), 50–52
  for Comforts Coconut Cake with Cream Cheese and
   Coconut Frosting (variation), 84
 Lemon Filling, 90
 Lemon Icing, for Gingerbread Cake (variation), 35
 Lemon or Orange Icing, 125
 Meyer Lemon Pound Cake, 79
Lincoln Log Cake, 105–106
Lindsey's Chocolate Cake, 87

Magic Spice Cake with Penuche Frosting, 96–97
Marzipan, 70
 carrots, for Carrot Cake (option), 44
 decorating with, 25
Meringue Shell, 89
Meyer Lemon Pound Cake, 79
Mixes, cakes made from
 Frying Pan Chocolate Cake, 40–41
 Pink Elephant Cutout Cake, 108

Nuts. See also Coconut
 Carrot Cake, walnuts in, 43–44
 to decorate with, 114
 The Elvis Cake, peanut butter in, 95
 German Chocolate Cake Icing, pecans in, 49
 Green Cake (Vert-vert), pistachios in, 117
 Marzipan, almond paste in, 70
 Pineapple Upside-Down Cake (option and variation),
  pecans or almonds in, 102–103
 to toast, 25
 Toasted Almond Brittle, 77

Old-Fashioned Banana Spice Cake, 74
1-2-3-4 Cake, 50–52
Orange Chiffon Cake, 31–32

pans
 preparing, 17
 sizes, to substitute, 13
party themes, favors, games, 59, 65, 108
Pastry Cream, 71
 for Cream Puffs (variation), 93
Pavlova, 88–89
Paw Paw's Birthday Caramel Cake with Caramel
 Frosting, 58
Peanut butter, in The Elvis Cake, 95
Penuche Frosting, 97
Pineapple Upside-Down Cake, 102–103
Pink Elephant Cutout Cake, 108
Pinwheel Cake, Bittersweet Chocolate, 119–120
Pistachio Cream, 117
Poppy Seed Bundt Cake, Buttermilk, 124–125
Pound Cake, Meyer Lemon, 79
Pralin aux Amandes, 77
Princess Cake, 68–72
Pudding Cake, Easiest Hot Fudge, 110–111

Ricotta Cheesecake, Aunt Frances's, 36
Rolled cakes
 Jelly Roll, 46
 Lincoln Log Cake, 105–106
Rum Toddy for a Cake, 85

Sauces
 Caramel Sauce, 93
 Fast Fudge Frosting, warmed, for Cream Puffs
  (variation), 93
Seven-Minute Frosting, 29
Seven-Minute Frosting (Fluffy Frosting), 122
Shortcake, Beth's Very Berry, 101
Spice cakes
 Gingerbread Cake with Chocolate Icing, 34–35
 Magic Spice Cake with Penuche Frosting, 96–97
 Old-Fashioned Banana Spice Cake, 74
Sponge cakes
 True Sponge Cake, 98
 Vanilla Genoise Layer Cake, 68
supplies and equipment, sources for, 127–128

Tarte Tatin (Benoît's Upside-Down Caramelized
 Apple Tart), 63–64
techniques, basic, 17–18
templates, 138–139
Texas Fudge Cake, Grandmother Whitehead's Famous,
 66–67
Toasted Almond Brittle, 77
True Sponge Cake, 98

Upside-down cakes
 Benoît's Upside-down Caramelized Apple Tart, 63–64
 Pineapple Upside-Down Cake, 102–103

Vanilla Genoise Layer Cake, 68

Whipped cream
 Cocoa Whipped Cream Frosting, 39
  for Cream Puffs (variation), 93
 Flavored Whipped Cream, 68, 101
 Lincoln Log Cake filling (substitution), 105
 to stabilize, 21
 Whipped Cream Frosting, 95
  for Cream Puffs (variation), 93
  for Jelly Roll, 46
  for Orange Chiffon Cake (variation), 32
  for Pineapple Upside-Down Cake, 102
 White Mountain Cake, 29

The exact equivalents in the following tables have been rounded for convenience.

LIQUID/DRY MEASURES

U.S.	Metric
¼ teaspoon	1.25 milliliters
½ teaspoon	2.5 milliliters
1 teaspoon	5 milliliters
1 tablespoon (3 teaspoons)	15 milliliters
1 fluid ounce (2 tablespoons)	30 milliliters
¼ cup	60 milliliters
⅓ cup	80 milliliters
½ cup	120 milliliters
1 cup	240 milliliters
1 pint (2 cups)	480 milliliters
1 quart (4 cups, 32 ounces)	960 milliliters
1 gallon (4 quarts)	3.84 liters
1 ounce (by weight)	28 grams
1 pound	454 grams
2.2 pounds	1 kilogram

LENGTH

U.S.	Metric
⅛ inch	3 millimeters
¼ inch	6 millimeters
½ inch	12 millimeters
1 inch	2.5 centimeters

OVEN TEMPERATURE

Fahrenheit	Celsius	Gas
250	120	½
275	140	1
300	150	2
325	160	3
350	180	4
375	190	5
400	200	6
425	220	7
450	230	8
475	240	9
500	260	10